WHEN PEOPLE PUBLISH

BOOKS BY FREDERICK BUSCH

Fiction

I Wanted a Year Without Fall
Breathing Trouble
Manual Labor
Domestic Particulars
The Mutual Friend
Hardwater Country
Rounds
Take This Man
Invisible Mending
Too Late American Boyhood Blues
Sometimes I Live in the Country

Nonfiction

Hawkes
When People Publish

❧ WHEN PEOPLE PUBLISH ❧

ESSAYS ON WRITERS AND WRITING

BY FREDERICK BUSCH

UNIVERSITY OF IOWA PRESS · IOWA CITY

University of Iowa Press, Iowa City 52242

Copyright © 1986 by Frederick Busch

All rights reserved

Printed in the United States of America

First edition, 1986

Jacket and book design by Richard Hendel

Typesetting by G & S Typesetters, Austin, Texas

Printing and binding by Kingsport Press, Kingsport, Tennessee

Library of Congress Cataloging-in-Publication Data

Busch, Frederick, 1941–
When people publish.

Includes index.
1. Authorship.   2. Authorship—Psychological aspects.   I. Title.
PN151.B87   1986   801'.92   86-7051
ISBN 0-87745-145-1

For my brother,

ERIC BUSCH

"She had an idea that when people want to publish they are capable—" And then she paused, blushing.

"Of violating a tomb? Mercy on us, what must she have thought of me!"

Henry James, *The Aspern Papers*

⋙ CONTENTS ⋘

⊰ ACKNOWLEDGMENTS ⊱

THESE ESSAYS appeared elsewhere, in altered form, usually sub-
stantially changed. I happily acknowledge the permission of the *New
York Times* to reprint parts of "Practical Love," which appeared in the
New York Times Book Review as "Fiction That's Glossier Than Life"
(January 8, 1984), © 1984 by the New York Times Company; of the
Chicago Tribune Book World for parts of "The Whale as Shaggy Dog"
(April 10, 1983); of *Modern Fiction Studies* for other parts of "The
Whale as Shaggy Dog" (*MFS* 19, Summer 1973); of *Ohio Review* for
"The Language of Starvation" (Spring/Summer 1976) and for much
of "In the Ossuary," which appeared there in Spring/Summer 1979 as
"When People Publish"; of *Seattle Review* for part of "In the Ossuary,"
which first appeared (Fall 1985) as "The Mont Blanc Pen"; of the
Washington Post Book World for part of "In the Ossuary," which first ap-
peared as "Spring Cleaning the Book Shelves" (April 4, 1982); of
Chicago Review for a section of the Preface, which appeared there in
1975 as "The Friction of Fiction"; of New American Library for "(We
Are Dead Now)," which provides the introduction for their 1984 *A
Christmas Carol and Other Christmas Stories*, and for "Holmes's Occu-
pation," which provides the introduction for their 1984 *The Sherlock
Holmes Mysteries*, both Signet Classics; of Viking Penguin, Inc., for
"Melville's Mail," which provides the introduction for their Penguin
Classic, *Herman Melville: Billy Budd, Sailor & Other Stories* (1986); of
the *Iowa Review*, in which "Melville's Mail" originally appeared; of
New Directions, for "Islands, Icebergs, Ships Beneath the Sea,"
which grew from my essay in their *A John Hawkes Symposium: Design
and Debris* (1977); of *Georgia Review* for "Even the Smallest Position"
(Fall 1984); of *Working Papers*, where in April/March 1983 a part of
"The Floating Christmas Tree" appeared; and of Gale Research Co.

for a part of "The Floating Christmas Tree," which in 1984 appeared as a portion of their *Contemporary Authors Autobiography Series.* My thanks to Charles Scribner's Sons for permission to reproduce lines by Hemingway; to John Hawkes for permission to reprint his work; to Leslie Epstein for his permission to quote from "The Steinway Quintet"; to Reynolds Price for his permission to quote from "A Word to the Reader" in *Things Themselves;* to Random House for permission to quote from *Ulysses* by James Joyce; and to Frederick Karl for permission to quote from his "American Fictions: The Mega-Novel" in Issue 7 (1985) of *Conjunctions.* Quotations from Norman Mailer's fiction in "The Whale as Shaggy Dog" are used by permission of the author and his agents, Scott Meredith Literary Agency, Inc., 845 Third Avenue, New York NY 10022.

◄§ PREFACE §►

THIS BOOK is about fiction writing from a writer's point of view. So it is in part about what happens when a novel or story reaches the public world (of publisher and reader) or doesn't. The essays are about the writer's interior world I ought to know best—mine. They are also ruminations about what other writers have felt or done, in private word or in further fiction making, when their efforts reached readers or didn't, or when other writers' work reached *them*.

Many of these essays were written because I admired a writer and wanted to say so. I think here of Dickens or Melville. I note that my admiration, sooner or later, becomes a meditation upon the fate of the artist or his book once the writing is done and the story is out, alone, in the world's literary weather. Speculations on Dickens, for example, run to considerations of his career, his own response to his history, and his expression of feelings about his past in terms of contendings with audience. An essay on Melville is, in this book, an essay on his relationship to publishers, magazines, reviewers, readers—and the powerful influence of Charles Dickens. If these essays were chapters in a work of fiction, I might call Melville and Dickens (and Ernest Hemingway) characters.

The book consists of my reaction to the force, beauty, fear and delight in several writers' work, and the travails and triumphs of the writers themselves. These are the essays of a writer studying writers, and not of an academic who seeks to purvey a system for reading or for thinking about fiction. (Though some of my best friends are academics who seek, purvey, read and think.) As a professor at Colgate who teaches fiction writing and the reading of fiction, I see my job as twofold: to help students learn to think about language, and to work at providing an audience for the Dickens or Melville to come (or those, unannounced, already here). These are not recycled lectures. I almost never use lectures, and my lesson plans are page numbers on index cards, prepared afresh for each day's class. I do not intend these essays as formal instruction, but as talk about writers and books among admirers of grown-up writing.

So the work that follows was written out of interest and, frequently, love. The essays are a kind of busman's holiday, worked at when I was recovering from, or avoiding, or holding off, for good reasons, the making of story- or full-length fiction. In the foreword to his book of essays, *Things Themselves* (1972), Reynolds Price describes that collection as "a book about waiting, some of the techniques of waiting." He says that "one of the most dangerous, permanent and generally ignored problems confronting any writer is how to use the time between books, between seizures." The essays in *When People Publish* might be described as time used by the writer; when he writes his fiction, he doesn't use time but does battle with it. Here I offer the work of an engaged noncombatant.

My writing about, say, Dickens is also about me as struck—the way the sea batters beaches—by Charles Dickens. My awe I reserve for the writers about whom I speak, but some of my attention, I affirm, is always for myself—as writer. I see Busch, the writer, as he is moved by the likes of Boz; and so these essays are always personal, just as they are always, at the same time, about the larger artist—Hemingway, Mailer, John Hawkes.

At this writing, I have published a dozen books and have written several more. I know a good deal about how writing is achieved, and it makes sense to me that, wanting to talk about that achievement, I rely on my own experiences. Doing so is, or ought to be, a refreshing change for a fiction writer. His job, as I see it, includes the omission of himself from his fiction. If I have much invested in my characters, the reasoning goes, and if some of that investment may be found in details from my intimate history and that of those I love or have loved, the writing is nevertheless about those characters, not me. It has to be. While a measure of self is essential to the psychic energy that fiction is pushed along by, an overdose is just that—poison for a story or book. Some of my hard work, when I try to write fiction, consists of saying, to the yappy, appetitious and insistent self, a surly *No*.

In the case of these essays, I have said *Yes*, and have talked about Judy my wife, my sons Ben and Nick; and I have talked about the act of making language, fearing its failure, loathing its reception: all first-person matters that one's fiction—it is always third-person, no matter the pronoun employed—should not discuss. Love and work are the subjects and obsessions of fiction writers, and here I talk *about* them instead of finding the energy for my prose *within* them.

There is terrible hard work in finding dramatic equivalents, metaphors of all and any sort—although each is similar in that it must satisfy the writer's *and* the reader's eye, and in vastly different ways—and these essays suggest my relief at having received my own permission to tell my tales *without* the necessary metaphors that fiction (and I) require.

Angus Wilson, whose art, wit, tact, scholarship and generosity constitute a gift to those who read and know him, refers to "our brothers and sisters in writing." While you might think him to be gesturing toward, say, Graham Greene or Anthony Burgess, he is in fact speaking of *all* serious writers. And so many of them are in this book with me because I have learned from my brothers and sisters about writing, and reading, and habits of work, and ways of watching the world and not just myself. In that sense, then, these essays come to their readers from a family of writers, while I, self-elected, step forward to make the mistakes and to hog what praise there might be.

The essays that follow, I have said, are a happy release for me from the search for just metaphors. But they ought to serve, still, in metaphoric ways. If, for example, I choose to celebrate James Joyce, and to think of his effect on me, and then to think of how he affected larger writers, I should nevertheless be suggesting—in an essay's structure, its voice, the information it presents—ways of thinking about writers and writing in general. The frictions of fiction, the ways in which texts influence writers, in which writers then make texts, ought to be considered by me in such a way as to remind me, and my readers, that such friction is not onanistic—that art is, because it is passionate and religious, about *the other one*, not self.

So I might begin—as I work to use my own history, and the strong presence of a major book, to speak about the shaping of language, I *should* begin—by raising the issue.

After masturbating on the Sandymount shore to the sight of Gerty MacDowell's thighs (I might say), Leopold Bloom, ashamed but not for long, says, "Still it was a kind of language between us." In that parody of romantic love and romantic fiction in *Ulysses*, Gerty creates

Bloom; he is her dream and a distraction from her life. She signals with her crippled body and her handkerchief, saying—making sure of it—that he is "a man of inflexible honour to his fingertips." In this novel of simultaneities, Bloom at the same moment is indulging in his own adolescent fantasy with his honorable fingertips, making her over into his dream of lust. The language between them is their captivity, and their illusion. I spoke a language like that to *Ulysses* once, and Joyce spoke back to me.

In Midwood High School in Brooklyn in the latter fifties there were people so ambitious and bright they were, it seemed to me, studying to attend Harvard and Princeton at the same time. While they skipped it altogether, I took a year to learn the one-semester course in algebra. I had flunked the geometry Regents examination (didn't bring a ruler or compass to the test) while they were giggling at calculus and worrying that their College Boards might keep them from exempting the first two years at Yale. So when one of those geniuses (now a *fakir* of the tapes for IBM) told me that *Ulysses* was a dirty book, I was determined to hot-hand a copy. After all, this same student had read Colin Wilson's *The Outsider.* He could define existentialism. And the East Sixteenth Street Branch of the Brooklyn Public Library had proscribed the book from its Young Adults section—proof positive, and positive lure: I could improve my mind and meet the nerve endings' needs at once. I would.

On a furtive Saturday morning, I rode the BMT to Greenwich Village and walked to the old Eighth Street Bookshop—when it stocked more mimeo'd poetry pamphlets than vegetarian handbooks. All the "real" Beats were asleep, and only the fakes—I wore black chinos (belt in back), black jersey, black shoes, I tried to look gaunt with vision—were leaning against walls projecting languor and the possession of inner truth. Having cased Eighth Street from the Greenwich Avenue end to The Cookery, I pretended to myself, in case I was being watched, that I had just thought "Oh: a bookshop. Why not pop in and buy a little Kant? And perhaps just a quarter-pound of Kafka. Don't bother to wrap it, thanks, I'll eat it here."

I foraged with red face and weak hands before all those ascetic women in turtlenecks whom I *knew* to be watching me—among Jack Spicer's *Billy the Kid,* and Ferlinghetti's *Tentative Description of a Dinner Given to Promote the Impeachment of President Eisenhower,* and *Howl,* of course, until I felt I had to make my move or falter. Past Denise Levertov, then, and Gregory Corso, Jerome Rothenberg; past Duncan and Blackburn; past *Visions of Cody* and Brother Antoninus—to that repository of license, the Modern Library. I stood before the Giants, pretending to myself—hence to the self-assured small man with salt-and-pepper goatee who looked as if he had just come from an early symposium on *Time, Its Future,* to stand before anthropology books but really stare at me—that I simply couldn't decide between a lot of Freud and too much Jane Austen. I remembered the cartoon I had seen at home, in an anniversary collection from the *Saturday Review of Literature:* a man blushingly walks through U.S. Customs with a giant oblong bulge in the back of his long coat; one officer says to another, "Poor guy. He thinks *Ulysses* is still banned." I simpered, I stammered, I dropped my eyes and then my change. But I had held it in my hands and had taken it with me in its plain brown bag: in 1958 I struck my blow for literature and sweaty dreams.

The book remained a mystery for forty-five minutes on the Brighton Local as I rode to Avenue H (I didn't dare take it from its bag on a public train). And then, in the kitchen, and then again in the hall, I had to make conversation, smiling animatedly, and not replying, and then replying too brightly, to something like "Did you take the garbage pails in?" Perhaps my parents suspected that something, so to speak, was up when I wore my pea jacket upstairs to my room. I persevered, and the secrets of a lady who was known to talk dirty came with me under my hot clothes. I locked the door. I sat on the bed. I opened the bright red book beneath its dark dust jacket—symbolism sufficient to that day—and I saw *Ulysses,* with an enormous *S* ending in *tately:* I wilted momentarily. For nothing so architectural, so full of purpose—I was an expert, had oozed over nursing handbooks and color reproductions of nudes in *Great Paintings of the World,* had skimmed every page of the purple-bound *Droll Tales of Balzac* with its breast-heavy woodcuts—could be a dirty book. But after paying my money, and having already worked my way into a sexual fret, I carried on. Through dialogue without quotation marks, and somebody laying snot on a rock, past some kind of play—I thought I saw something good there, but I was hurrying for more substantial provender to feed my beast—and then to "Yes because he never did a thing like that before"; good times felt closer, an hour had passed, my head was aching because I hadn't wasted time in turning on lights. And then, exhausted, I found "considering how big it is so . . .": *triumph!* Joyce spoke over my shoulder, and I spoke back in the rhythms of my fevered youth.

Other hours in other days were devoted to turning up the fellatio reference by Molly, and doglike copulation, and the deliciously disgusting tongue-seven-miles-in-hole, and every other truffle within sniff. Eventually, when I had learned from my parents that they considered the book respectable, *Ulysses* went from the top of the closet to the forthrightness of my shelves—between *Navy Diver* and a paper edition of Samuel Shellabarger's *Captain from Castile.* It came out only for frictional emergencies when I was home from college and too full of myself. I read it halfheartedly, under a weight of astonishing ignorance, before I graduated from college. And then, years later, when I was ready, I read it in three days of awe, once actually shivering, and often calling aloud.

I would like to sentimentalize my churlishness by saying that Joyce would have appreciated my introduction to the book he drove himself and his family into for seven years. But he was not only Poldy and Henry Flower smirking over thighs that twinkled on the shore. He was also Stephen, Jesuit-manqué and pronouncer of his own approaching fame. He might, if anything, offer "Behind. Perhaps there is someone," and walk off into his future.

"Someone" is all of us. And still we assemble separately—writers and readers—on Bloomsday, June 16, which is a moveable feast, to ask

> What spectacle confronted them when they,
> first the host, then the guest, emerged
> silently, doubly dark, from obscurity by
> a passage from the rear of the house into
> the penumbra of the garden?

and then to once again admit, and lament, then celebrate that we could not arrive without Joyce at the answer: "The heaventree of stars hung with humid nightblue fruit."

Hemingway complained (in a section of "Big Two-Hearted River" which he wisely pruned before the story was published) that "Dedalus in *Ulysses* was Joyce himself, so he was terrible. Joyce was so damn romantic and intellectual about him. He'd made Bloom up, Bloom was wonderful. He'd made Mrs. Bloom up. She was the greatest in the world." In *To Have and Have Not* he made his admiration clear.

Faulkner denied the influence of *Ulysses*, saying that Joyce was "a case of a genius who was electrocuted by the divine fire." Yet according to Mrs. Faulkner, "When we were married . . . he began what he called my education. He gave me James Joyce's *Ulysses* to read. I didn't understand it. He told me to read it again."

So I have talked about Joyce's frictions against other writers, including myself, have discussed what happens when people (in one marvelous case) publish. I should, for the sake of accuracy and honesty about notions of literary connectedness, note that Faulkner wrote the screenplay for *To Have and Have Not*. I should say that he excised most of the Hemingway and all of the Joyce.

Joyce studied Dickens, and I study the work of Joyce and of Dickens, and others—for example, Reynolds Price. Each of those three wrote and writes about the dreadful difficulty and heroic effort of getting through the separateness, the dark, impermeable barrier that surrounds us and separates us one from another. Each wrote and writes in praise of what we do for one another—*to* one another—in our effort to come close. Writers when they read may often reach toward other writers, in their work, for sustenance during the desperate moments of formulating stories. When I write, I look back into myself, of course, but do not tell you outright. In these essays I can, and, in the case of James Joyce, did; I skipped the dramatic metaphors that fiction would require, but surely—see how I said what I said about the terrible separateness in which I unhappily believe—I meant those nine paragraphs as metaphoric.

And so I mean this book. I hope that it doesn't suggest everything I know about making fiction, because I am greedy and hope I know a great deal more that I haven't yet discovered how to tell. But I hope, too, for students of writing and for serious readers, that it suggests ways—lots of ways, useful ways—of reading honest books honorably, and of thinking about how writing gets done.

Writing is the hardest work I know, outside of loving another human being. While I wish for my fiction to deal adequately with the labors of loving, I hope as hard that these essays may deal to someone's satisfaction with the love involved in writing well.

◄§ IN THE OSSUARY §►

THE PUBLIC LIBRARY of my boyhood was seven or eight long blocks from my home in the Midwood section of Brooklyn in the 1940s, and I walked past fresh-fish markets, and a stall run by a woman from Poland who spoke no English (and needed none) when she sold homemade pickles and sauerkraut, and past the open-air shop that specialized in knishes and charlotte russe sold in paper cups. The Woolworth's I passed had long floors made of boards that creaked, and there were bins of lead soldiers. And in the library, upstairs over apartments off Avenue J, in a neighborhood of immigrants and the children of immigrants, I learned about books.

Books were on shelves that, in the children's section, were no higher than my stomach. Books were made of wartime paper that yellowed at once, that smelled of vanilla and of the steam-heat that misted the windows. The floors creaked like the floors at Woolworth's, and books were found after one tip-toed along the planking's creaks and groans that rhymed with similar sounds from behind other shelves. Books were what I carried home and upstairs. Lying with my head at the foot of the bed, the door to my room shut, lying in the light that came through huge old maples and oaks—the light was always green—I was above the backyards, above the world, out of it, really, and in the pages of what I found at first by accident, then because I wanted them again and again: *Navy Diver*, by Henry Gregor Felsen; a science-fiction book, whose author I've forgotten, called *Angry Planet*, in which kids went to Mars and fled large polyps under a red sky; *Captains Courageous*. Books, then, were part of the old warm busy neighborhood in which few enough of the adults read anything; my parents were among the exceptions. In the nonprofessional families, books were for children, somehow, they were for dreaming on, and for later enacting in games. For me, they were for solitary browsing, for solitary reading, for the isolated imagination in which most verbal children live.

Now that I write books, and teach them, and press them upon my own children, I find myself in the lugubrious frame of mind so common to the adulthood of such children as I was. I understand that if books are to be my livelihood, they must be sold. As publishers become, each day, further pressed to make profits—by a crushing economy, by the conglomerates who annually make books part of a process in which cars, soapsuds, and dolls that excrete must be sold in large quantities—publishers are forced to care less and less about the dream I have tried to suggest. In place of the dream that starts with the word, publishers are required to try to feed the appetite that exists, the dream that someone else has begun.

Gothic romances, then, and books on how to run and how to live without love; books of information—how banks work, the history of Seattle, the origin of massage parlors—whether they are called "fiction" or "fact" have replaced what I once thought books were. Nonprofessional readers and students buy what they're driven, by films, television and word-of-mouth, to buy. They take from libraries, for the most part, what they're too stingy or poor to buy, but what they would buy if they believed in purchasing books. Publishers like to offer books for which there's a market. With film and television tie-ins, or in response to the appetites created by movies and TV, they offer versions of best-sellers, responses to sexual politicization, answers to the major question of the decade: "How do I *do* it?"

Surely, publishers and readers are pleased by the literature that is published, in small quantities. We are all happy, I suppose, that short fiction collections are brought out by Knopf, that Atheneum has an estimable poetry series, that New Directions offers European fiction and poetry (before it is discovered for classroom use, or before it is a trendy item). The publication of literature is still exceptional, however. I remain grateful to those brave houses who printed Sartre and Shaw so that, as a junior high school student, I could find them in my public library and start my life with serious writing.

What is published is, more or less, what will sell. Perhaps it has always been the case, if to a lesser degree. But the library, anyway, was the place I went to for what was *written*, not for what was selling. It was the dark continent; it was the place for discovery. I think this no longer is the case.

Librarians are overworked and underpaid. Their process of selection is such that they rely on a very small number of sources for advice on what fiction and poetry they should acquire. They rely on *Publishers Weekly* and the *New York Times Book Review*, on the Kirkus Service reviews, and on a few professional librarians' journals. The ethic among librarians is that they serve their patrons—not that they suggest, through their choices, what their patrons consider. Surely, in the days of general public insistence that tax dollars be spent in response to the public mood, the ethic must meet with approval. But the combination of selection tools and service-to-patrons has significant results. Among them is an end to those steam-heated, floor-creaking dreaming days in the old library.

Spot checks, for example, are conducted in many libraries. At a prearranged time, certain members of the staff visit certain areas of the library's collection. If specific books are not there, then multiple copies of those books are purchased. Thus, the patron is served. Thus, some libraries will own six, ten, twelve copies of *The Thorn Birds*, or novels by Danielle Steele. Is there much demand for *Major Barbara*? Not according to the spot check. Further checks of circulation may reveal that *Major Barbara* hasn't been taken out for two years. When it's time to weed—and in days of limited space, of the ever-increasing publication of books, of purely logistical problems, weeding has become a crucial function in libraries—then *Major Barbara*, or Elizabeth Gaskell's *North and South*, may have to be weeded; it may be stored where a wandering child might not readily find it; it might be sold for fifty cents at a library sale to raise money for what patrons increasingly demand: best-sellers, how-to-do-it books, or audio-visual materials. (School libraries are more and more called Multi-media Centers; tapes, cassettes, computers, video cartridges, book-and-cassette sets are on the rise in libraries. Guess what is in decline.)

With what space and money remain for serious literature—and I am hardly demanding that all of a library's space be given over to it— librarians, many of whom have no particular love for poems or short stories, many of whom have received little or no education in their qualities or their historical value, must make choices of what to acquire. They read *Kirkus Reviews, Publishers Weekly*, and the *New York Times Book Review;* they read them not so much, if at all, to find out what may be superior and engaging art, as to find out what their patrons will be demanding. While the *Times* may sometimes, even often, be less commercially oriented than *PW,* its overall interest remains in what is popular, or in what books certain publishers and writers have made large financial or other investments.

So what does the librarian order? Perhaps what *Kirkus* recommends: "It's all here: the Holocaust, international intrigue, a wicked step-father, sex and fraud. . . . a snappy tale with enough entanglements for TV or film." The book is an autobiography. Perhaps the librarian will consult *PW.* How does *PW* do its advising? In italics, beneath its Fore-casts: "Playboy Book Club dual main selection. First printing 50,000; initial ad budget $35,000. Author tour." Patrons will see the author on television, will see ads; *they* won't have to buy the book in response to the TV appearance and ads: their library will do it for them. And in place of an un-*PW*'d first novel, or an unnoticed book of poems by a farmer from Maine, the library will purchase a book that is praised, as one in *PW* recently was, because "readers are assaulted with crooked cops, incestuous father-daughter doings, drug-dealings, beatings, Cuban plots and such." *And such.* It is the *and such* factor, the you've-seen-it-on-*Miami Vice*-and-*The Edge of Night,* and-you'll-love-it-on-your-Mexican-vacation factor: from *Playboy* and TV and drive-ins to the library. And because the librarian is trying to satisfy his patrons, *not* because he is opposed to art.

But he isn't supposed to support and promulgate art. The result, despite whatever beneficent motives, is the same. Our libraries are being plugged-in, friends. They are extensions of what Paramount Pictures think Simon and Schuster, and Pocket Books, both of which they own, ought to be selling. Paramount Pictures is owned by the Gulf & Western conglomerate. What have they, what have Paramount Pic-tures, produced that convinces you their motives are for holding back the darkness? And for whom, to whom, is *PW* written and published? It is written for the publishing trade. It is directed to book stores, to help them decide what to purchase. And what will most bookdealers buy? Quite obviously, what they will sell. Libraries, then, are becoming adjuncts of that side of the profession: they are becoming tax-funded bookstores. And whatever convinced you that book publishers and bookshops, nowadays, are holding back the darkness, or are trying to, or think it much of a necessity?

Is what I've been calling "serious writing" *about* holding back the darkness? Is that what fiction and poetry are about?

No. They are, in fact, about my father, Benjamin Busch, who, while serving with the 10th Mountain Division during World War II, in the Italian campaign, was wounded by fragments of a land mine. Ernest Hemingway, he explained to me while I was in college, had written about being wounded in terms that were doubly meaningful to my father after his legs and hand and groin were, to various degrees, torn by shrapnel. This was in 1958, and I had brought home from Muhlenberg a clumsy short story. My father read it, set it aside, and told me, "Very nice." He meant to be kind. But he meant more to go on—and this is what he did—to tell me about his wounding: how the officer ahead of him had been torn apart by the mine's explosion; how he himself had thought at first that he was dead; how men carried him down a rough mountain track, setting the stretcher on the ground and protecting him with their own bodies when shelling from the German mortars became too accurate; how, when he could, he reached down to his groin and brought his hand up and, seeing blood, thought at once of Jake Barnes and *his* wound, and how he would be required to act with Barnes's grace now that he was maimed.

Benjamin Busch, whole, came home to Brooklyn to father a second son and to rejoin his law firm. He had nightmares about the war, and his wounding, and he didn't read Hemingway again except, I think, when *The Old Man and the Sea* was published, and when Hemingway sent those sad reports of his sentimental journey to Spain. He didn't want to read Hemingway, and he didn't want to read much else that was what he called "unhappy" or "make-believe." He stuck to books about the Dead Sea scrolls, and Bruce Catton on the Civil War, anything published about Lincoln, and analyses of the politics of Wilson, Roosevelt and, after a while, Ike.

And he does so, I believe, this eminently practical man of law and business, because he is a real reader. He was so moved by Hemingway, had so made Hemingway's language part of his own life, that in the most dangerous instant of his days, he thought not of God, or his mother, or me and *my* mother at home in the States, but of Jake Barnes: because in the "make-believe" of *The Sun Also Rises*, Hemingway had created such truth that my father felt it as actual during his critical seconds.

Surely that is why he rejects things "unhappy" or smacking of "make-believe" in books: when they work, and when he reaches far enough into them to help them to work, he becomes frightened. For my father has tolerated too much reality: it tried to explode him. The reality of "make-believe" exploded him in another way. He was so very much like Nick Adams after his—Hemingway's—war, in "Big Two-Hearted River"; listen to Hemingway describe Nick's prayer: "He felt he had left everything behind, the need for thinking, the need to write, other needs. It was all back of him." The story proves "it" wasn't; "it" was with Nick nearly all the time. And "it" was with my father.

But there he sat, folding his large hands, and asking me, my little story now ignored by us both, whether I were truly serious, as serious as I said, about wanting to be a writer. I replied that I was. (How did I *know* that?) And my father told me, then, that I would need to know two things. "First," he said, "it's a terribly long, hard haul. People will try to ignore you and they'll try to hurt you if you keep them from ignoring you. What a writer needs most is energy. It's the most important thing you can have if you're really going to be a writer and outlast the bastards who'll try and stop you." He almost never swore, and the "bastards" stunned me more than the advice itself—the importance of which I cannot overrate. "And second is," he went on, "You have to write dialogue. Nobody will believe your stories unless they have dialogue in them. People *talk*," said my father, who so often didn't. "You should read Hemingway. Did you ever read Ernest Hemingway? God. *The Sun Also Rises* is a beautifully written book. Did you ever read it? There's a lot of dialogue in it that you could look at. You end up believing it—it's very moving."

For a man who sometimes didn't want to talk, or who felt discomfort in talking intimately, it was a pretty long speech. And for a practical man, the man who had given up his painting, who, like other practical people, was moved to tears by Ezio Pinza's rendition of "Some Enchanted Evening," the man who no longer read things "make-believe," the giving of such advice was, to me, an astonishment. Now it isn't. I know now how very vulnerable and how always-wounded he was. But then, in 1958, what he said was somehow extraneous to what I'd known of him. But, and in spite of my ferocious lack of insight, my father's words sounded undeniably true.

I read Hemingway. I went to his books as if to school. I still do, sometimes. No one could convince me not to. And I think that in my father's recollection of artful words made flesh—Jake Barnes, his injury—lies the key to what "serious" writing is about. It is dangerous writing. It makes us, with out secrets and lies, hurt. It doesn't keep the darkness out. Nothing so safe: it lets the darkness *in*.

Like nearly everyone else, I have been telling stories since I was a very small child. I continued to tell them as I grew up, and I haven't stopped. While I was hunting for a title for a new book of stories, recently, I realized that after all those words I still had never told myself what a story actually is.

I know that a short story is prose, that it is fiction. Some or all of it is made up, or is made different from something I've actually experienced, seen, or heard. I know that it's a *story,* a narrative that moves through time while attempting to move the reader in the same direction as the events I offer through description and dialogue. I know, too, that each detail, sound, act of the narrative, is intended to make the reader think and feel *more*. While he moves with the grain of my words, he must also move against them—as if he strokes a child's hair backward—so that what he reads offers him more than one sensation or thought. I offer him *child,* but because of the context and method I achieve, I want him to simultaneously apprehend: *Oh, her child,* and *Why does she abandon it?* or *Why must it die?* or *How well it dares to live!*

So a story has to be about something that matters. It therefore has to be about people—the people in the story, and the significance in them for the people outside the story who read it. Thus, it is required that I respect the people outside the story. Which I can do only by respecting those within, my characters.

Stories are called "short stories." They are smaller than novels, smaller than novellas. We're talking, then, about made-up narratives concerning movements in time, the motion made by people who matter, for people who matter. All right. But *why* are stories smaller than novels? Of course, the answer seems obvious: they take less time to happen. It isn't that less actually goes on so much as that less time is required in the narrative itself.

Which begs for argument, one like this: if Joyce's novel, *Ulysses,* covers the events of a single day, and if his story, "The Dead," takes much of a single day, why isn't each a novel, or each a short story?

Because "The Dead" and *Ulysses,* though each reviews a life through various telescoping and amplifying images and acts, see time differently. Into Leopold and Molly Bloom and Stephen Dedalus, in *Ulysses,*

Joyce pours the fullness of three lives, and a sense, at least, of the civilization behind each life. While in "The Dead," Joyce wants Gabriel Conroy and Gretta, his wife, to see their own lives through a very few metaphoric instants. In *Ulysses,* he shows us the texture of lives in many small details. In "The Dead," he shows us a few weavings, a very few designs, and uses them to suggest the rest. In *Ulysses,* Joyce wants to slow the day into slowest-motion, to examine the essence of a great many feelings and perceptions. In "The Dead," a very few incidents and utterances are used to channel us with some speed toward the sharing of Gabriel's vision: that love is lost to him, that his life is like a death.

Short stories, I am saying, offer less; what they offer is designed to unfold in our minds so that the less becomes very much more. A story gives selected details in order to suggest a whole life, while a novel can pretend to give—make us believe we're receiving—very nearly all the details of a life in order that we see, and feel, and understand it. Stories imitate our ancestors' cave-fire tales of risk and learning; novels imitate their epics of tribal migration and the cycles of their game and crops.

I wonder if the story-teller isn't less like the novelist and more like the poet. He begins, it seems to me, as the poet does, in the ossuary, where the bones of the dead are laid down. It is the pit in which remains—evidence—of life are either set in a shape that helps to pray for something better (for the arrangers as well as the arranged), or into which the bones are dumped because somebody wants them out of sight.

Like the poet, the story-writer contemplates those bones in Yeats's foul rag-and-bone shop of the heart. But instead of telling whose body those bones come from, and where the body originated and, possibly, what he or she ate, and where, and with whom, and for how long—this is traditionally the novelist's work—the poet and story-writer select one bone's shape, one suspicion of a single meal, a sense of one fellow-diner, and through action and conversation meditate a brief unit of the bones' humanhood into plausibility.

Of course, the poet has all the advantages. Story-writers must imitate poets as well as they can. The poet has the music of compression, the space between the lines and words. In the poem, you can hear the singing of what's left out. It's the startling energy of stars that roars in the radio between stations late at night. That emptiness is full; it contains our intimations and inferences.

The poet has melody too. Again, story-writers imitate him as best they can. He can sing death, like Galway Kinnell, until we understand that people are heroes for starting, with death's breath in their faces, to love. The poet can carve the precise stone steps of memory, like Philip Levine; he can celebrate the climb up, the undignified fall.

All this the story-writer wants to do: make shapes through the power of what can't be said, or what mustn't be; make music in the world of facts. But because he wants to say *And then,* and *Then,* because he wants to say how bodies move in space as well as time, the story-writer's music and silences are cluttered with cloudy jars of half-used grape jelly in lukewarm refrigerators, flapping flat tires on cross-country trucks, the mechanics of slowly opening doors.

I think this is true for most story-writers, and I know that it's true for me. Triggered by guilts and lost delights, by the need to explain and celebrate and make actual in the actual world what is metaphor at first, or of my dreams, I write stories about creatures who move in space as well as time and in my mind. I'm a colonialist, like most fiction writers; I want to take what I can of the verified world, then render the world I inhabit inside, and make the two worlds seem to merge. And, having tried to create that verisimilitude, I want to capture boatloads of convicts, rejects, runaways, the fittest of the unfit, and transport them toward my Australia or America, my new world they're fooled to want to settle in.

And yet I want that music too, those magical silent spaces. Failed poet and front man for the penal colony, I settle for what I can get: the melodies of stuttering speech, the faked expressions of mostly made-up people whom readers think they actually see, the song inherent in the fighting-through of people who share a room or house or bed or child or journey: they fear to perish of one another, or without each other, and yet, calling each other dead, they won't lie down.

Several years ago, I started, immodestly enough, calling some of my stories "domestic epics." Writing to friends, I tried to tell them that what I worked on were small moments, or shaped selected collections of moments, in which a significant measure of wonderful human adventures were enacted in small, metaphoric ways. I never thought I was offering *War and Peace* in thirty pages. But I did think I was suggesting that the hugeness of that tragic adventure, or of *Our Mutual Friend*, or of *Losing Battles*, could be found—little but essential—in brief fictions.

Lawrence did it in, say, "An Odor of Chrysanthemums," Hemingway in "Big Two-Hearted River," and Cheever, and Updike, and Raymond Carver, Grace Paley, Albert Murray, Cynthia Ozick, Andre Dubus, Rosellen Brown, Tillie Olson, William Gass, and so many others. They had the need and energy to think big and little at the same time. Reynolds Price's "Waiting at Dachau" contains the palpable loss given off by poetry, the motion across time and space of a novel, all made—you can very nearly hear the spade grating into gravel and roots—in a perfect shape: the grave's.

As those writers, and so many others, are heroes to me, so too is the nature of their endeavor. They work in no-man's land, where the language seeks poetry and extended narrative at once. Short stories are, in fact, the long and short of it. Books of them are very often difficult, harder to read than novels. Once you forget your armpit-sweetener, your car's rusting rocker panels, commit yourself to a novel, adjust your vision to it, hear language in its terms, you can be carried by the flow of narrative and lose some hours profitably. But in a book of stories, you're forced to adjust, then readjust, then readjust again, and each revision of your vision is a dislocation, the breaking of a small bone. People would rather forget their cars and deodorants once than break a dozen small bones.

So I return to bones, the one with which I've been banging my drum, and the ones I claim are source and substance of the stories I write and admire. I have a title now: *In the Ossuary.* It may not be the one I use for the book at which I'm worrying, but it's useful for a great many story-books collectively. It suggests that from the faulted skull and puddled ribs, a story-teller can fabricate the illusion of actual flesh with hair and lifelines on it; and someone will care about how that skin and skeleton crossed on the earth, and will learn or simply feel, now differently, about his own pacings back and forth. And maybe, then, that is what a story is: the ossuary, where life enfleshed by language starts again.

In 1970 and 1971, from September through February, Judy and Ben and I lived in a thatched-roof cottage on the edge of the Salisbury Plain—or, rather, on the edge of the hamlet of East Winterslow, which sat on a hill that overlooked the plain. We fancied we could see South-

ampton and the sea from the flint-and-brick cottage, the topiary garden, the little row of apple trees. Ben, eighteen months old, in blue
MotherCare play suit and red rubber boots, grazed among the fallen
green apples. And we used to rush to a narrow front window that overlooked the lane when Lady Coleman rode by, in high black boots and
high black hat, on her chestnut mare. Hilary Sandle, who rented Lilac
Cottage to us, had told us that Porton Downs—where the Defence
Ministry was said to manufacture poison gas and other weapons—was
not too far away; but "they're really very quiet," she'd said. Stonehenge
was half an hour's ride, and we went there several times a week. Ben
used to clamber on the long, low stone where, we were certain, Tess of
the D'Urbervilles had slept, watched by Angel Clare, until at dawn,
from every point of the compass, the sheriff's men came riding to take
her to Winchester, where she was hanged. Ben called Stonehenge "Da
big wocks."

We had seven thousand dollars for air fare, hotel in London, the
used Austin 1800 sedan we bought, the ninety-four dollars a month
rental on Mrs. Sandle's cottage, fifty pence a week for chirpy, stout,
and generous Mrs. Cowshall who cleaned on Wednesday mornings,
then took Ben to play in town with her grandson while we saw local
sights; there was enough money to permit us to travel to Scotland, the
Lake District, Ireland, and into London for a party given by the publisher of my first novel. Somehow Judy sneaked money out to surprise
me with a Mont Blanc pen, a narrow cousin of the great fat ones ad-
vertised in the *New Yorker,* but still four and a half inches long, almost
an inch around, jet black with a long gold point, and the sort of foun-
tain pen a writer starting out should have—a nod toward real crafts-
manship, a demand for competence, a sign of faith. It came from Har-
rod's and remains a tool of great importance, and a crucial souvenir.

The pen is in my hand now, its extra-fine tip made soft and leaky by
a little boy who needed it for drawing dinosaurs on rough construction
paper. I used it nearly every day after I received it. I wrote stories,
made notes for stories—I had completed a novel and was trying to
produce a volume of short fiction—using the Mont Blanc pen and
thirty-six-pence notebooks purchased at the W. H. Smith in Salisbury
(which steadfastly refused to stock my just-published first novel).

With that pen, which drew narrowly, leaklessly—youthfully—I
wrote the drafts of stories never published and of stories not completed, and of one or two that almost worked. Nothing I wrote in those

seven months was, finally, worth keeping. I typed my final drafts on a huge, ancient Underwood, shaped like, and nearly as heavy as, an upright piano. It was lent by Les Pennels, Mrs. Cowshall's son-in-law, whose automobile shop was a great, dark barn made from timbers taken from a scuttled ship of the line, the wood for which had been hewed a hundred years before in the nearby New Forest.

On most mornings I rose very early, made coffee in the small tiled kitchen, and went to work in an extra bedroom. Judy rose later, when Ben did, and though her coffee was warming, so was Ben. The bedroom in which I worked overlooked the garden. It was black on autumn mornings. The pigeons chirred and rustled in the thatch. And I wrote stories. They were about men in their late twenties and early thirties. They were about men with women not that different from Judy Busch. They were about parents of men like me, and colleagues of journeying assistant professors like me, and beautiful American babies like ours. They were etched in fine lines that spun out precisely from the Mont Blanc pen which now, as I write about the past, and not the present of which I wrote in 1970, lays down lines that ooze a little, spread, and lose the tautness of their intended shape.

It is that way with stories and story-writers too. I think how Irwin Shaw, after *Tip on a Dead Jockey*, wrote fewer and fewer stories. I think of John Updike, who has published fewer stories in recent years (or so it strikes me), and who has in recent essays inquired—and not, I think, rhetorically—why Hemingway wrote or published stories less frequently as he aged, and then not at all.

Part of the answer may lie in Hemingway's reflection that in his early days in Paris he was writing stories the way one runs short sprints—in preparation for the longer race. But when he was a novelist—after *The Sun Also Rises*, and after *A Farewell to Arms*, after the long books about bullfighting and the African hunt, he wrote great stories. Some of them—"The Gambler, the Nun, and the Radio," "The Short, Happy Life of Francis Macomber," "The Snows of Kilimanjaro"—were extensive, divided into virtual chapters, and otherwise informed by what Hemingway had learned about shaping novels.

But they were stories nevertheless, written lyrically, in response to fairly recent experience. They contained remembered elements (as did his early short fiction in *Three Stories and Ten Poems* and *In Our Time*), but they were clearly provoked by the writer's very recent responses to very recent (interior) events.

After a while—after the stories of bad wealthy people and the noble plain folk Hemingway admired and never, finally, could be; after the African stories about men who'd sold themselves short (and out)— Hemingway had caught up with himself. By 1938, the writer who was born in 1899 had dealt with his past—fictively—in terms of a lyrically evoked present. He was middle-aged. He had written about boyhood in his young manhood, then about aging young manhood, then about earliest middle age, and then he looked about to find himself in a vigorous time but with—suddenly, it must have struck him, and shockingly—a prelude to growing old on its way. Real time had caught up with him. Unless he chose to record honestly, in fictive terms, the travails of being Ernest Hemingway and suddenly hating time, he would have to return to the past. He eventually fled to *A Moveable Feast*, about his youth in Paris. And he made a lot of it up.

I don't presume to know John Updike's life, and I have never met him. But he is celebrity enough for a reader to guess about the shape of parts of his domestic history. After his splendid, moving stories in the *New Yorker* about the divorce of his characters, the Maples, and about its aftermath, the number and (for me) the brilliance of his short stories has somewhat diminished. There is a recent story about being famous—in the story, it is an actor who is famous, and who is also artistic and conscience-riddled—and a reader might feel that Mr. Updike is edged up on by actual chronology, and not the past examined, felt, in terms of recent history.*

And after such impudent speculation here I sit, scattering ink across the page, writing about East Winterslow in 1970, and not making fiction. I called the Mont Blanc pen a souvenir. Perhaps I should have called it *memento mori*. Not, of course, that one necessarily dies if he writes fewer stories, or none. But one does die *away* from his fiction if, as a mature writer, past the first novel, he writes only novels. For, however personal their content and concern, they are shaped—they

---

*Updike, in an interview with Mervyn Rothstein (*New York Times*, November 21, 1985), says, "I had both the happiness and possible misfortune of very early getting into print. . . . And having been a writer now since my early 20's, there is a danger of getting written out and even becoming stale." He goes on to say that "you use up those first 20 years of your life one way or another, and the material you collect in adulthood doesn't have that—it's not that magical. You have to give it magic. You have to substitute wisdom and experience for passion and innocence."

must be—according to a character's, or to characters', demands—the demands of life-on-the-page as it shifts and wriggles and evolves, *becomes* what, some years and hundreds of pages later, it wants to be about.

A story, though, is short enough to be subservient to a writer's commands. It too will take on life of its own, of course. But its brevity permits the writer to enforce his will—which, often enough, is his need: to reflect, to synthesize, to lyrically *say.* He is there, in his stories, and we find him. He might find himself. When he doesn't write stories, he is lost in his longer fiction—to nosy readers like me and, again, to himself.

Some writers therefore write short fiction as if driven—John O'Hara was one—because the present activates and galvanizes the past, because whole speech now is like needing now to fully breathe. Whether or not the pen writes cleanly or the ink will sometimes stray, some writers work at short fiction because it is made of mysterious moments of realization, or implosions of the sense that something is present to be understood. It says in shapes of event what will not stay still to be spelled out. It is as puzzling as life can be, as incomplete as life can feel, as lithe and in-process as life must seem—to those who are, one way or another, puzzled or yearning, or possessed by the notion that they are not done.

On my wall is an underexposed color photo that Judy took in Lilac Cottage. Ben stands on a chair at the kitchen window and looks up at me. Our faces are close, and I am bending down. I have hair on my head, which now I don't, and Ben's hair, now dark, is blond in the picture. His fat-cheeked face says that I am at the least absorbing, and possibly wonderful. My face is a shadow, a shape of glasses and beard. I wonder what its expression is. When we stand in that relationship today, Ben, seventeen, is three inches taller than I. He bends down to me. So I come here alone to bend at my desk. I spread the misbehaving ink around. It wanders, it runs. And Stonehenge now is surrounded by scolding signs, by fences and by gates, and nobody's baby can dance on the stones.

A friend of mine who writes novels, and who for years has (somewhat) jokingly referred to himself as an "upstate obscurantist" because his work is poetic, and not always available to the reader's first knock, announced with some surprise a while back that he is increasingly interested in telling stories in his fiction. I said with a similar proud surprise that I was too. Since we had agreed to take turns as New York's leading upstate obscurantist, and since like most writers we favor in conversation a drift toward that perilous shoal, the self, we had a long and all-too-flattering discussion of ourselves and the idea of story.

Reynolds Price, whom I consider one of the bravest, most dedicated and most interesting writers in America, has for years maintained that the essential endeavor of fiction writers is the making of story. Toward that end, as well as because he has been trying to understand and use his Christian feelings, Reynolds has even transliterated and translated Biblical passages: they tell stories; they are, he says, the heart of narrative. And narrative is the process he wants us all to understand.

So I and my fellow former obscurantist talked about our separate yet parallel courses, edging ever closer to the hull-busting *I,* and names such as Reynolds' were brought up repeatedly, those whom I saw (and see) as caring for precisely wrought and poetically evocative language that nevertheless serves a narrative drive: the *and then* of literature. I tried to synthesize, like a historical revisionist: James Joyce, whose *Ulysses* I once loved because, I claimed, it eschewed story, I now praised because Joyce told stories through his twenty-four-hour poem. I now claimed under the flag of story telling Melville's *Moby-Dick,* Dickens' *Our Mutual Friend,* Lowry's *Under the Volcano,* Nabokov's *Lolita*—masterpieces, once, of texture and resonance and verbal play, now for me were all of those, and were, in addition, first-rate examples of how stories might be told.

My friend pointed out that in five years I might possibly be a full-time obscurantist again, full of love for the nonstory of *Finnegans Wake;* and I agreed that we see, so many of us, in order to serve the nature of our vision. So many writers are unreliable critics, over the long haul of a career, because we nurture our craft and art by fictionalizing the nature of fictions we read, in order to support the requirements of the fictions we write, or want to write.

Thus ended our night's conversation, and it was a good one. But today, I am alarmed at what I said (and what I think essentially true). For most writers, or at least many, are also teachers in colleges and universities. We cannot make enough money from our writing to support ourselves and our families; the schools are our patrons, and we owe them service—advanced courses in graduate English departments or postgraduate writing programs, undergraduate seminars in

contemporary literature or Milton, and, all too often, crowded lecture
courses in American or English literature from Then until Now. And
in performing our chores—in buying summer months, and sometimes
even mornings or parts of weekends for what most of us consider our
realer work—how do we repay our patrons?

It seems to me, it is possible anyway, that while we often tell "the
truth"—evaluate, say, Dreiser in a historical and critical context, and
read him unselfishly on behalf of our students—we might as often lie.
As fiction writers teaching Dreiser because he is in the syllabus, we
might make claims for him that we don't believe. That is no great sac-
rifice: it doesn't hurt the students to read him, and to think about him
as a great American artist. It could also be a kind of lie, though. And
what of a teacher-writer's realer enthusiasm—Melville, say, or Joyce?
Claiming either as poet one year, and as story-teller another, do we
wreak damage? I'm not sure, and I do wonder. Surely, we writers are
not different, in some ways, from full-time English professors who
loved Hemingway once, then began scorning him because the current
sexual politics denounced him as unworthy of women. And there is the
growth factor: we, too, learn as we teach; and we change our minds.

But students sometimes want to believe what writers say about writing. Like it or not, we sometimes have an influence—usually, and la-
mentably, outside our writing—and we must be mindful that classroom ways of talking, and what we do on the page, while nourishing for
us, may not be wholly useful to our students. Which makes for, at the
least, a greater tension between our academic and artistic lives. It's fine
discipline for us to have to read and talk to bright young people. But I
think it would possibly be better for all concerned if we taught a good
deal less. Or taught classes called Prejudices I and II. And got paid,
like other working folk, a fair wage for what, on the page, we have labored to make.

But another issue involving story-tellers (even antinarrative writers), and the academy, and those scourges and necessities the publishers, is becoming clear to me. There is a recent, frightening WE in
business, and its perils are more barnacled, fog-shrouded and destructive than any *I* in the conversational shipping lanes.

I refer to the WE on whose behalf Professor Frederick R. Karl
writes in *Conjunctions: 7*, published in the summer of 1985. Espousing
a theory about something he calls the "mega-novel," the large books
of—to name two—Thomas Pynchon and Joseph McElroy, Karl says

the usual about what has come to be called post-modern fiction: that it doesn't deal in character or social structure or language that is "clear-cut" or "unambiguous." Instead, the mega-novel distinguishes itself "by its inconclusiveness; its lack of closure; its self-conscious languages . . . its determination to evade resolutions; its resistance to social and even political and cultural ramifications; its determined deconstruction of novelistic materials."

In spite of the jargon, one can see such a statement as more of the usual, and one can agree or disagree. But then Professor Karl saws off his shotgun. Setting up the good novelist William Kennedy as his straw man—it isn't Kennedy's fault that most of the recent literary rings have fallen to his fingers—Karl characterizes Kennedy's Albany novels as "short, readable books in the minor mode, hybrids of American tough guy fiction." "We should have moved on from there a long time ago," Professor Karl says, speaking for us all, or at least those of us who carry mega-novels to the classroom in our briefcases.

I also refer to the WE mentioned on the front page of the *New York Times Book Review*, when John Barth's *Giles Goat-Boy* was published in 1966. The reviewer, who was about to participate in a major financial venture—a writer's success, a publisher's harvest, the remuneration of countless bookdealers, and sizeable library expenditures—was a professor. He said, "Barth makes few concessions to the dull or the uneducated—to the 'plain reader.'" This can be a good or bad quality in a novel, and it needn't be either praise or damnation. But note what Professor Scholes went on to say: "For some time we have been wondering what to do with the training given us by . . . giants of modern fiction, wondering whether we were really meant to expend our hard-earned responsiveness on such estimable but unexciting writers as C. P. Snow and Saul Bellow." This is said by Professor Scholes on behalf of a novel in which, to quote his summary, "the universe is reduced to a university."

That WE, of course, need not necessarily have included only college professors, other people do read difficult texts for pleasure. But you know, and I do too, that the bulk of that WE is, surely, composed of English teachers and writers who don't, always, teach in order to live. And the readers whom Melville sought (and lost), the readers whom Dickens was able, nearly always, to win, were ignored—were meant to be—by that formulation. It embarrasses me. It frightens me, too. For it implies that the range of serious writing is circumscribed by the campus's perimeter: the "Revised New Syllabus" of Barth's novel censors, through Professor Scholes' scorn, those texts that people of imagination, not educated by him and his colleagues, might care to read or write.

It was for me a most visible beginning of a pattern of recent intellectual aggrandizement. It continued for me in a statement by the critic and professor, Richard Gilman. In 1975, reviewing Reynolds Price's novel, *The Surface of Earth,* on the front page of the *New York Times Book Review,* Professor Gilman wrote from the Northeast that "there is no present Southern literary art of any distinctiveness, any special energy or élan," thus eradicating Price, Crews, Walker Percy, Eudora Welty, Cormac McCarthy, Gaines and others, in one simple stroke. He went on to pronounce that "we've been under the sway of the more or less detached, ironic, cool and essentially unlocalized American literary intelligence and vision." Naming Pynchon, Barth, Hawkes, Barthelme and others, Gilman argued that because the WE have been "under that sway," because of critical or commercial *trends,* Price's novel was to be scorned: "Who could have imagined that any novelist presumably sensitive to the prevailing winds of consciousness . . . could have written a relentless family saga at a time when most of us feel self-generated, inheritors of obliterated pasts?"

Most of "us" do not feel "self-generated," in fact. We may say that we are, when we try to describe the effect of a certain number of books by certain writers at a certain time; and of course we are really trying to say what the overall effect may seem to us to be. But as *people* do we really feel self-generated? Not unless we are amoebas. There's a stink of classroom and Ph.D. dissertation on those "prevailing winds," a rank smell of small fashion. (Where was Professor Gilman when John Hawkes was writing his early novels and receiving so little public support?) How "self-generated" do "most of us" feel when parents sicken or die? When we see old friends or recollect lost loves? When our children want to forget us? Such easy statements as Professor Gilman's ignore, or want to, the actual emotions of the human creature, and the thousands of poems, stories and novels—some by Hawkes, Barth, Pynchon—that are brave enough, needful enough, to confront the past. Professor Gilman's "most of us," like Professor Scholes' "we," is a red herring and an arrogance, and a considerable misapprehension.

The WE is the corporate literary version of the military-industrial complex, no less. In Professors Gilman and Scholes (and so many others who are professors, critics and authors at once), the WE becomes an announcement that decisions affecting the relatively many readers and writers are made by the few—who form a nexus of power by whom decisions are made when, conceivably, they might be made by others who are *not* academics living in intimate relationship with review journals, publishers and universities. New Haven, Providence, Ann Arbor and Chicago all have come to Dunsinane—or at least to New York.

Readers had a difficult time obtaining Price's novel after that scandalous growl of the WE. What bookstores would stock it? What publisher, except the most courageous, continues to promote it? What teacher of contemporary literature lectures on it? Some did; too many didn't.

Both Scholes and Gilman are interesting, and they are often brilliant. I think each should have known better than to replace his judgment with the taste of the WE. I continue to respect them, if anyone cares, and do not wish to make either the target of this rumination. But I do want them to serve as emblems of a danger faced by readers and writers in this day of conglomeratized publishers, books published because Book-of-the-Month Club suggests their publication (and promises adoption as a Choice), chains like Waldenbooks (whose decision to sell a book, or not, can make or break it), and review sources that are oriented toward bucks and not beauty. The academy, the publisher, the book dealer and the reviewer have drawn closely together; there *is* a literary-academic-commercial complex. It endangers the teaching, perhaps the writing, surely the publishing and reviewing, of venturesome books. Is it true that we have met the enemy and he is WE?

One of our sons asked Judy, after hearing me use the word, what "plot" meant. Without pausing, and without hinting that Aristotle once walked, she answered, "What comes next." I've come to rely on that definition.

Plot, as a factor in fiction, *is* what comes next. Plotting is the building into a fiction that sense of necessity which causes the reader to want to know what comes next, and which makes the reader feel that what has come to pass in the novel or story is necessary. Thus, in *David Copperfield*, it is plot when Mr. Murdstone marries David's mother and becomes his oppressor; it is plotting to offer the event with enough verisimilitude to make the reader feel that the awful event is inevitable in the context of David's life—and, furthermore, that David's life could not take place on the page unless that event took place.

By contrast, the plot seems merely convenient—one might, on such occasions, even want to use the word "forced," or call the circumstance pasted on, merely useful to Dickens' purposes—when Mr. Micawber goes to work in Uriah Heep's law offices. The action is forwarded, the characters are brought together, and the novelist can clinch matters conclusively. But we do not feel that it is in Mr. Micawber's bones—that it is purely necessary—when he takes the job. Dickens loved his characters, and although it was necessary *to him* (certainly, that is always half of the novel-writing battle) that Micawber be in a position to thwart Heep on behalf of Aunt Betsy and Agnes, it does not feel necessary for Micawber, as character, to take that particular position. Dickens believed, and in his soul I think, that the world was a network of interconnected lives, an enormous ganglion the strands of which met, separated, crossed and recrossed, always to meet significantly at last. Sometimes, as in the case of Mr. Murdstone, or in Quilp's pursuit of Nell in *The Old Curiosity Shop* (that implausibly persuasive novel), or in the identity of the stranger in *Our Mutual Friend,* one feels that it is a function of character that coincidences occur: lives in which we want to believe do coincide. Possibly equally often, one feels that the appearance of Bounderby's mother, in *Hard Times,* or the identity of Oliver Twist's mother, and her relationship to the kindly Mr. Brownlow, are insisted into eventuality, and do not have an integral relationship to the nature of those characters on whom the plotting hinges.

Superior plot, then, to my way of thinking, is a function of character. Character is made through action. The way a character acts in the world tells us who he is. And the way his author forces him to act—the plot—is persuasive and moving (in effect, the *rhetoric* of character), and revelatory of the nature of his world, in proportion to how well an author can shape a person on the page whose response to the world feels necessary.

Tolstoy subordinated his characters' actions, in *War and Peace,* to historical necessities. Yet Pierre and Natasha are the people who, given their circumstances, must act that way. History is a character for Tolstoy, and the manner in which he creates that world to which his characters are forced to respond determines the success of his plot.

That is the manner in which Hardy, forcing coincidences in, say, *The Mayor of Casterbridge*, makes us feel for Henchard. It is not only the depths of Henchard to which we respond, but the meticulous rendering of a place and time—a world in which such enormous things happen. So too is it with Conrad's people. And that is why, though we can live with Marlow, and eagerly follow his life's path as it moves to intersect with Kurtz's in *Heart of Darkness*, we are finally unpersuaded by Kurtz (his impact on the Marlow we accept), and Kurtz's Intended. They, and their actions, are insisted; Marlow is inevitable.

When Reynolds Price's second novel, *A Generous Man*, was published, it was clear to most readers and writers that Price's sizable impact upon present-day writing was undeniable. Still, not a few critics were nasty toward this novel's mythic qualities. Milo Mustian, a boy on the verge of manhood, hunts for his dog. His dog has run into the wilderness in pursuit of an escaped circus snake named Death. I cannot recall a review in which mention was made of the inevitability of such a pursuit, *given the nature of Milo*. A plot such as I have sketched, such a triggering action, can be made to sound implausible, even absurd, particularly in an age when randomness is celebrated (like a disease it is important to have had) and the impossibility of coherent plot (like the "impossibility" of happiness in the Twentieth Century) is proudly stressed. Though the donnée may require a deep breath for some, at first, the shape of the plot does not—given the nature of Milo. Character is action. Milo is an attractive character, verisimilitudinous; his life circumscribes him, and he would give much—including, perhaps, his safety, his stability, his life—to achieve, if for a while, some sense of larger possibility in what time is left to him by circumstance. And since Price makes the world to which Milo reacts a dark frontier-place of dreaming, where history visits our interior selves, the novel, for me, works magically.

Price came close, though, to that line between insistence-upon-events and superior plotting. I have elsewhere called him brave, and *A Generous Man* is an act of intelligent courage. Price obviously felt that he needed to risk the reader's disbelief because he had a story he needed to tell. And perhaps in this context it is time to think about the nature of story, its relationship to plot.

I earlier called story the *and then* element of fiction. But that sounds dangerously close to Judy Busch's definition of plot: what happens next. Are plot and story the same?

Most people don't say "story" nakedly. They link the noun to its familiar preposition: "of." Lord Olivier didn't, in his film, describe what was to follow as "Hamlet's story"; he said, "This is the story of a man who could not make up his mind." And it's worth noting that the "of" linked the familiar hodge-podge of interpretations, guesses and bewilderments to a precise clue to Hamlet's way of being. Olivier told his audience that story is how you acquire hints about a person's fate, why it occurs. "Hamlet's story" might be the plot alone—its events and outcome. "The story of a man who . . ." is the *how* and *why* of a plot.

So the story of Gretta and Gabriel Conroy need not be the plot of Joyce's "The Dead." The plot lies in the intersection of people and events, the relationship between the past and present—in superior fiction, the future too, of course—that events help us to see. The story is in the nature of the characters—what in them makes us want to know more, what makes us understand or feel more: about them, and finally about ourselves. The plot takes Gabriel, after hearing his wife talk about her dead lover, to the window, where he sees the snow burying Ireland, and his own dead life. The story is Gabriel's insistence—we have this archaeological instinct in common, most of us, to bury and then unearth—upon first ignoring the essence of his wife's history, then his insistence upon plucking it from the tomb and digesting it into his own blood.

Another insistence should be mentioned too: Joyce's insistence upon telling us, upon making a design of events such that we want to know, then do know, as much as Gabriel wants to know, then does know. Joyce was obsessed, as all good writers are obsessed, with the need to *tell.* Reynolds Price named a snake Death, and set into motion a series of events risky to a second-novelist because he had to talk, and in such a way as to tell us otherwise unsayable truths.

Just as Adam, or Cain, or the Wandering Jew, or Melmoth, or Viktor Frankenstein or his creature were cursed to wander and tell their tale, so is the writer obsessed, a voice wandering in search of a listening ear—or an ear available to be made to listen. This is no romantic notion of the blighted artist (though Romantic artists surely held the notion). It is the starting point of fiction: a voice that must tell its story. For story exists not only in relation to the events on the page, but as a function of the voice driven to create plot so that its world-of-the-page and its characters can intersect in prophetic and revelatory ways. Coleridge's Ancient Mariner breaks into domestic coziness by interrupting a wedding party, fixing the guests with his crazed eye, and saying, in effect, "Listen to me: I have a story about events and people—me—whom you cannot imagine, but shall." Melville, in *Moby-Dick*, starts with his story-telling protagonist button-holing the reader, ends up with him surviving to need to tell his tale, and in between has him invent—again, *tell*—much of what transpires among Ahab and the crew, while Ishmael is nowhere near those acts or conversations. Lowry, in *Under the Volcano*, is a grave-robber: he is so compelled to tell his story that he brings back from the dead a man compelled to tell *his*.

The story-teller, I'm saying, is driven to make shapes you are driven to study—they are composed of his characters' lives and the events of his characters' world. He makes a plot in order to do so. The examples I've suggested are not the names and achievements one often hears, nowadays, in connection with story. When a present-day writer makes a book full of predictable sex, melodramatic considerations, much action, lengthy to-ings and fro-ings, and characters translated from—or soon to be translated to—films and television, his publishers, and all too often his reviewers, call him a "master story-teller."

That phrase today, I'm afraid, more often than not means this: "Here is the work of M. M. Kaye, Jeffrey Archer, Leon Uris, all those scriveners of tales about car factories, banks, airlines, churches, synagogues, tempted priests and rabbis' wives, the typists of *romans à clef* about movie stars and millionaires—here is a writer who is not driven to make a language evocative and resonant, because that would tax you, discourage you from buying the book, and frighten newspaper 'critics'; here is a book full of information about events or institutions that have recently been in the news, a book about superficial matters, with a plot more or less plausibly tied together; here is great length, because you want a big fat read for the airplane or because you have nothing else to help you keep reality at bay; here is a book that will not frighten you unless you require cheap thrills; here is *no* reflection on you, no news about you, no requirement that you reconsider your assumptions about yourself; here is a book to talk about the darkness, but to keep it attractively distant."

Those "books" are for "adults," those who need to be screened from what Melville called "the blackness of darkness." Children, for whom story is as basic a need as love, particularly small children, while they will watch nearly anything on television that is violent and stupid, are attracted to stories that are mythic, risky because they concern threats (abandonment by parents, say), and true to the sense of dire possibility that lies in superior plotting. Our children understand the possibility of story in a snake named Death, a stepfather named Murdstone, a man named Henchard who would sell his wife and leave his baby. "What comes next" is what their lives are about, and the needful voice of the story-teller, demanding that they see how lives in the world-of-the-page can intersect, is what they hear and what they want to hear. *Hansel and Gretel* is going to outlive the collected works of Victoria Holt, and our children can tell us why.

My wife, a patient person but also a librarian, told me at last that her ultimatum was this: I must weed the books on the floor-to-ceiling shelves in my workroom and in our bedroom, or she would do it herself. The threat was considerable. Librarians can be cold of heart. And while they might, at times, insist that they were placed upon the earth to help people locate and be pleased by books, they do also enjoy getting rid of books.

Books that don't circulate are weeded out. At library book sales, I have bought, for pennies, books that you might want to call precious, or wonderful, or at least all right. For reasons unknown to me, *The Sun Also Rises* didn't circulate in a local public library. I purchased it for a quarter. The cloth binding is black, and on a golden label, pasted onto the front of the binding, Ernest Hemingway's name appears under the title. The paper is good; it is, of course, stitched, for the book was made in 1926 by Charles Scribner's Sons, when the art of book manufacturing was more important to show off—or more feasible. On the front title page, there is an engraving of a more or less Grecian goddess or very attractive mortal, sleeping or stuporous, leaning against an olive tree; I think I see pipes on the ground beside her, and an apple—some forbidden fruit, surely—half-held as she slumbers. I remember saying to a hard-working and devoted librarian, "Hemingway could have touched this book. People who were young when he was, who were discovering him while he was discovering himself, who are living in town right now, *did* touch it." My local librarian agreed, as you might agree with a strange, large dog who suddenly erupts into yapping. I have the book, and I have my convictions about it and old books in general: they are like out-of-date coins, talismanic in their usefulness. I have saved many of the great predecimal pennies of England's 1920s, all retired in 1970. Like them, books are a kind of currency; they touched people, and people touched them. It seems wasteful and destructive to throw away the coin of history, over which actual lives have made friction, leaving invisible cells.

According to librarians, and therefore according to my wife, you risk such waste when you have to. Apparently, I had to, so here I was and here I am, trying to weed my library. I have just come upon our triple copies of William Saroyan's brilliant first collection of short stories, *The Daring Young Man on the Flying Trapeze.* When I was learning to write fiction and allegedly attending graduate school, in late 1962 and early 1963, I came upon a few books that changed my life, and this was one. It showed me how lyrical and personal and conversational and from the overfilled heart one might make a story. It helped me want to be a writer more, and it showed me what I might do to become one.

In our shelves are the 1961 paperback edition from Bantam Books (fifty cents), yellow at the core of each page, brown along the edges, and falling apart because I used the book hard. There is an English edition that I bought from a bin in a supermarket in Salisbury, Wiltshire, because I wanted a copy near me in Lilac Cottage in 1970, and because it amused me that the English published such an American voice at all, and then dumped the book in a Tesco Market bargain bin just as the Americans might. And then there's the edition I found discarded on an airport seat in North Carolina not too many years ago; I brought it home because I was afraid that Saroyan soon would die, and I wanted to honor him by at least rescuing his book from the ignominy I felt he suffered in his final years.

Weed, I am told. Certainly, I reply to myself, alone with these books. Shall I discard the history of the Bantam edition? Or the sense of delight and nostalgia that cling to all of the books we acquired during those seven months in Lilac Cottage? Surely not. Then discard the airport copy, I instruct myself. Why be soft? Keep only two copies of the collection, and don't mollycoddle yourself.

But then I look through the copy I'm to discard, and I come upon Saroyan's story, "A Cold Day": a poor writer, freezing in San Francisco, plans to take his cheap, second-hand books and burn them in a bathtub to keep himself, if not comfortable, at least warm enough to survive. He reads a passage from one of his soon-to-be-burned books. "Now that isn't exactly tremendous prose," he decides, "but it isn't such very bad prose either. So I put the book back on the shelf." And so do I. If Saroyan could freeze for his books, or make a protagonist who did, then I am not going to throw away a page on which this character shivers. Three copies of the Saroyan, then, will remain on our shelves.

We own two copies of Schwartz-Bart's *Last of the Just* and two of Leslie Epstein's *King of the Jews*. One is the copy we read and wept over, the other is a lending copy for friends who ought to be reading the book. You can't weed out your lending copy; not even a librarian would force you to do that, I tell myself, and I move on.

Our beloved professor at Muhlenberg, Harold L. Stenger, Jr., taught Shakespeare, and he spoke better wisdoms about that language than I have since read. We don't really need two complete editions of the plays and sonnets. But what if he said something in my wife's class that he didn't say in mine? How can we risk losing those ideas, written onto small margins in a crabbed collegiate hand? Save the Shakespeare, I instruct myself.

And probably, I tell myself, save the multiple copies of Thomas Hardy, some of which we read in Macmillan cloth editions in England in 1970–71, and some of which we reread in Papermac editions in England in 1974 and 1978. The same is true of the Dickens from those years—Chapman and Hall editions, Penguin editions, Everyman editions, each of them the locus for an emotion and thought associated with a place and time we've moved along from. And how could I toss out the contemporary fiction I bought while we lived abroad, no matter whether I failed to read it then, and probably will fail to read it now or in the near future? Some of it—for reasons of the marketplace, for reasons, too, of quality—is absolutely out of print. Does one, I ask myself, extinguish perhaps the last flicker of an author's presence-on-the-shelf simply because the shelf is a mite crowded? Save Peter Everett's *The Fetch* (in Penguin) and the Peter Owen edition of Lillian Halegua's *The Hanging*.

Keep *The Traitor*, purchased for twenty-five cents a few years ago, even though it was published so unattractively by Grosset & Dunlap in 1907. Thomas Dixon, Jr., its author, also wrote *The Clansman*, from which *Birth of a Nation* was adapted. If possible, this book is even more villainously racist than *The Clansman*. Keep it though you despise it, I instruct myself. Show it to students. Keep it to hate.

Keep two identical paper editions of *Wuthering Heights*—there are three more on the shelves in the college office, each with different marginal notes—because you think it's a wonderful book and, while you were reading it once, you actually called out to your wife, *"Amore!"* Keep two copies because you're a fool.

Keep multiple copies, also, as tokens of your love for the author: Hemingway (at least six different editions, including one facsimile, of *In Our Time*); Faulkner (four copies of *The Sound and the Fury*); Graham Greene (three of *The Heart of the Matter*); Ivan Gold (an Avon edition of the 1963 *Nickel Miseries*); and so many others. Keep the books, I instruct, because they are tokens of history, actual currency of times that have passed; and therefore the books, in a way, are as precious to have as times now lost to all except the mind. Keep the books because you're a writer who wants to be saved by someone's slovenly shelves. Keep them to preserve what might not be printed again. And keep them because your children might one day read these shelves and find a record—an artefact made of these artefacts—which can tell them something of you and your interior times.

Save the lot of them, then. When you weed a garden, you tear out the less pretty, the wilder, the more aggressive, the generally untamed. But such characteristics are what one often writes books about. You often, I remind myself, look into fiction for just such beings—less pretty, wilder, generally untamed. So let the garden grow disheveled. Celebrate the weeds because you want to celebrate the people in those books and behind those books and the people of this house, and what they've loved.

We live outside a town called Sherburne, in upper New York State. Boys and girls go barefoot there in summer and part of the fall, and they fish, build tree forts and ride bikes. Many of them learn about their bodies in haylofts. Some of the children go to college, though more go to a nearby two-year agricultural school, and many of the parents are farmers, truck drivers, clerks in a college yearbook factory, janitors and secretaries at Colgate, twenty miles away. The girls tend to get pregnant early, the boys tend to join the military, and the television sets flicker for most of the day, go off early at night.

Sherburne seems to be a typical American town. There is one black family in it. There are no Orientals. A little boy in a nearby town told us how his parents had taken him to the State Fair, in Syracuse: "We watched the Jews a lot. You should of seen the Jews." Few folks show when a hardy little chapter of the KKK burns its cross. And if there's a

fire or a flooded house, the women gather to watch the men in the
Volunteer Fire Department wear and use the latest equipment in re-
sponding with pleasure to emergency.

Saul Bellow, of course, won the Nobel Prize some years ago. The
New York Times Book Review, the *New York Review of Books* and most of
the periodicals read by serious writers and readers did, in one way or
another, mark the event. Of course. Even the Utica and Syracuse papers, which are essentially vehicles for the wire services and supermarket ads, carried small articles. But the newspapers printed in the
immediate area of Sherburne did not: it wasn't news of the order of a
major commercial-block fire in Norwich, or a change in the Hamilton
zoning laws. And if I stood in the center of Sherburne and if I screamed,
for an hour, at the top of my lungs, "Saul Bellow" (or "García Már-
quez," or "Isaac Bashevis Singer"), my townsfolk would think, first,
that I was describing a new disease—*Saul*bellow, a cow affliction, or
Isaacba*shev*issinger, an exotic rot on corn—and then, second, they
would think that I was as crazy as I'd seemed.

That is literary fame. It doesn't mean anything outside an inner core
of some book-club memberships, literary readers, professors and writers—and not too many of them get all that much of the literary news
all of the time. Most of us know how little financial reward there is for
most writers. Most of us know that the best write because they're compelled to do so, and by needs they cannot price.

If fame, money, recognition—some sort of authorial currency—is
denied writers, and they know it, most of them, soon enough, then why
do they write? A famous editor remarked once that writers' stories are
analogous to the drawings you bring home from school to show (and
woo) your mother. Surely, there are many editors who will tell you that
writers are damnably like little children. And it may be that I am always
making things to coerce from my mother some praise.

But I wonder if there is not something equally childlike, or at least
rooted in certain patterns of child's play, that might be more instructive. I think it is found in my sons' building castles of plastic Leggo
bricks, in their designing intricate self-sufficient worlds (on drawing
pads, with rocks in a field or on a beach, in their verbal play) of which
they can be wholly the gods. I think of the map of Yoknapatawpha
County which the author drew for Malcolm Cowley's *Portable Faulkner:*
"William Faulkner, Sole Owner and Proprietor," it said, and that
ownership extended to the *populace,* remember. Children and writers

make such worlds and, to the degree to which they are burdened by care, imagination, dilemma or an unspecified need to escape, yet simultaneously cope with, what is actual, they delight in the making of the alternate world, the controlling of its every breath and detail, and the offering of it, momentarily, on loan, to those who live in the world called "real."

Think of Hemingway as a boy, late at night, reading by flashlight, over and over, his *Robinson Crusoe*. In it is a world apart from the world; in it is every detail labored over and specified—created; in it is the island of imagination: a troubled place, and lonely, it is nevertheless a place where the tyrannical imagination of Defoe, or the reader, can exert control, and be a king. When I was young, I'm told, I was found reading simultaneously three copies of *Robinson Crusoe*, which I'd laid out side by side on the floor of my room in Brooklyn. When I was asked why, I answered that Crusoe had dropped his knife, at one point, according to the edition I'd taken from the library. I wanted to check, I said, to see whether in another version he might have remembered to pick it up. That knife would have to wait for its recovery until I wrote my own moments of sought-out yet stranded solitude. A character pocketed it for me in *Invisible Mending*, in 1984.

Think of Dickens, the boy, first hearing and then reading the adventures in *The Arabian Nights*. Those strange countries were always used, in his novels and stories and letters, as metaphors, and as models of feelings of being separated, away. Setting his books in the center of London, or the north country of England, or France, Dickens made places that were simultaneously recognizable as real and as wholly off any map. He made the London of the mind, as did Hemingway with his Michigan or Paris or African jungle—as did Conrad with *his* African jungle.

So the writer, I suggest, exerting control, then relinquishing enough of it to allow us a peek; making places that are recognizable, yet far away and even almost impossible; making people who can live in the actual yet also invented world; wishing for audience, but not willing to do for it what it alone demands; lusting for reward, but remaining adamant that the willed word be foremost in consideration—the writer, then, may be, indeed, very much like a child.

Except that the best of them, I hope, are unlike children in this respect: they know full well what they do. They understand how there is little victory for them—mercantile or popular—except in the making. This sounds wholly idealistic, and therefore untrue. Perhaps it will sound truer if I add that writers are still enough like children to grumble and grouse—I do so in these pages, surely—while understanding that the only *real* reward is in the making. They catterwaul because they hope against hope for what grownups get: cash, praise, assurances. These are what they *think* the grownups get. And all the while they have what they never entirely wished for and never can be rid of: the need, and sometimes even ability, to make a shape from the bones of the dead whose grave they rob; the need and sometimes ability to make a gingerbread house in a forest of shadows; the need and ability to place in that landscape a person or persons who, for even a little while, will seem to have flesh on the bone and who will seem to breathe and speak the language of hoping against hope—why not call it prayer?—and who, given enough time, will do exactly what the writers, if the writers are lucky, say.

❦ THE LANGUAGE OF ❧ STARVATION

EATING IS a political act, in fiction a political metaphor. Suicide by starvation is a vote—perhaps an act of war.

Eating is literally performed by a child in a functioning family, or by an adult who, metaphorically a child, receives bread (or the money that buys it) from the parental state or institution. Eating is a function of enablement, of somehow being fed. And eating is an act ranging from acquiescence to subservience, whether or not there is gratitude involved. It acknowledges the feeder's ability—superior power—to provide the food.

So to reject the proffered food is to reject the feeder—to proclaim to parent, institution, state that it is *not* transcendent: that its body and blood do not substantiate. Intentional starvation starves the feeder of the signs (and pleasures) of power. To intentionally starve is to repudiate and wound the world, to reverse the customary flow of psychic force by the grossest of physical means: starvation by preference is rebellion which succeeds.

Some of our supreme fictions make use of this political metaphor. Often discussed as literature of alienation, they are rarely referred to as political. Yet Melville's "Bartleby" is as political as Thoreau's "Civil Disobedience"; Kafka's tale of family horror, *The Metamorphosis*, is as political as *The Grapes of Wrath*. Each reveals that the modern hero can triumph over the world only by dying away from it. Our literature is not only concerned with death, but our heroes—those who win out over the world's thrall and terror—must die, not survive in wounded courage, to defeat our enemy—the age we have made. Survival is *not* victory. The metaphor of suicidal starvation will perhaps suggest ways of seeing how that sad vision works.

For example: the fiction of Henry David Thoreau, in which his character Henry David Thoreau, pictured as an embattled prisoner—in no danger whatsoever, and really knowing it—mocks his jailers with their "foolishness" for treating him as if he were "mere flesh and blood and bones, to be locked up." He repudiates the notion that the human spirit can be enclosed and says, "I was not born to be forced. I will breathe after my own fashion." That fashion presumably includes the ultimate option: not breathing at all. Although we assume that Thoreau was not suicidal, we cannot assume that his literary persona was unaware of his power, through death, over life. For he says, "If a plant cannot live according to its nature, it dies; and so a man." It is a threat of refusal to be wrongly nourished by a wrong world.

One reason for the appeal of "Civil Disobedience" to present-day readers is the modernity of Thoreau's imprisonment. It is not so important that he thinks himself important for defying the state. And it is not important, even, that he thwarts the state until he is bailed out. What matters, and what is so modern, is that Thoreau, who should be a victim, decides the quality and degree of his victimhood: he insists on the primacy of the self. *He* decides that it is his jailers who are captives, not he; *he* decides that a work of art about his victimization is a weapon against diminution; and *he* decides that a man in prison may die by the most dramatic and metaphoric way, if he chooses. The victim, then, controls his response to the state's control. He is no longer a nineteenth-century hero who watches himself be disposed of. He makes an artwork of self-disposition as he preaches "Disobedience to Civil Government" and loyalty to self-government. No wonder Gandhi saw the essay as a weapon deadly to empire.

Gandhi's phrase "passive resistance," which does not occur in "Civil Disobedience," does occur in Melville's "Bartleby, the Scrivener. A Story of Wall Street." The story, published in 1853, five years after Thoreau gave his lecture, is of course read as a metaphoric tale of alienation. We need only recall the architecture of the nameless narrator's law chambers to verify such a reading: the chambers are on Wall Street, walled off by surrounding high buildings; half opens on a view of darkness, half on light; the two clerks, Turkey and Nippers, are complementary halves, one a fury of passions and inefficiency in the morning, the other in the afternoon; the lawyer's room is walled off from theirs; inside his room, a screen separates him from Bartleby; behind the screen, Bartleby stares through a window in a "dead-wall revery" at a wall of bricks. Clearly, the story is concerned with separated parts of the self, with being walled away from one's realest self, and from the world.

But it is also a story of political subversion and starvation. Paid to work for a bastion of the establishment, a man "not unemployed in my profession by the late John Jacob Astor," Bartleby subverts the workings of the law firm, drives the lawyer from his own offices and into "fugitive" wanderings about New York—and perhaps into recognition of his own humanity—by saying "I prefer not to." By forcing society to hear a preference, instead of witnessing mere refusal, Bartleby forces it to acknowledge a statement of taste and judgment—hence the fact of the whole human being behind the statement. Esthetics here becomes political weaponry.

Bartleby then reinforces his succession of preferences-not-to—his suggestion not only that he *is* because he refuses, but that not-being is preferable to that world which is—by starving to death. By refusing meals which the lawyer bribes a warder to give him, Bartleby rejects the world ("I am unused to dinner"), denies its ability to nourish him, and removes its power to do so. By facing his prison wall (forcing the lawyer to feel shut away—the jailer jailed) Bartleby, echoing Thoreau's proud rhetoric, establishes by his death that he is robbing the state of its power. He makes the biggest protest, states the clearest preference, compels the world to acknowledge who he is and what he wants by forcing its representatives to dig a hole and place him in it. And he makes a metaphoric prison of the world which survives him.

For Kafka all the world is a prison, and it is not certain whether he makes his family a paradigm for that world, or the world a model for his family. Part of his greatness, probably, is that the two are so interchangeable: he is an artist of the very narrow and the huge at once. The body of his work is a study of power and powerlessness, and here is how he describes family love, in his *Diaries* for November 12, 1914: "Parents who expect gratitude from their children (there are even some who insist on it) are like usurers who gladly risk their capital if only they receive interest." Emotional nourishment is extortion, and this is Kafka's revolution against it:

> The parents and their grown children, a son and a daughter, were seated at table Sunday noon. The mother had just stood up and was dipping the ladle into the round-bellied tureen to serve the soup, when suddenly the whole table lifted up, the tablecloth fluttered, the hands lying on the table slid off, the soup with its tumbling bacon balls spilled into the father's lap.

That entry in the 1914 *Diaries* shows how much Kafka saw eating—the family communion—as political, and how much he wanted the tables turned in his family, which he loved and which dominated him and which he feared. It is how he saw the world.

The same family group appears in *The Metamorphosis*. Trapped in his room, Gregor Samsa rebels and locks his family and employers out. He is the world's victim, and he denies his body to its appetites by changing so utterly that he no longer satisfies the hungers he once did. He is abandoned (freed) by family and employers. The metamorphosis, effected by his buried rages, removes him so far from the world that his own appetites can no longer tolerate that world. He starves away from it, repudiates it, and achieves his emancipation; he is now called "the thing next door," is freed even from invocation by name.

At the beginning of the novella, immediately after his transformation, "He could almost have laughed with joy" at the sight of bread and milk. Eventually, he puts food in his mouth when he happens to pass it: he "kept it there for an hour at a time and usually spat it out again." At the end, Kafka merges spiritual and physical with his evocations of food: "Was he an animal, that music had such an effect on him? He felt as if the way were opening before him to the unknown nourishment he craved." Although Kafka uses the language of eating, his character speaks of music, not food. He has already made "the decision that he must disappear," and he is beyond corporeal nutrition. The language reinforces what the rejection of food has already told us: that Gregor votes against the world by leaving it.

In "A Hunger Artist," of course, the focus of the story is starvation itself. While it is a parable of the artist and his needs, it is also an enactment of the artist's political desire—to force the parental world to respond to him, perhaps even love him: the hunger artist says, "I always wanted you to admire my fasting." Kafka goes beyond Melville in creating political protest and in analyzing it; the artist here is helpless, the revolutionary feeble, before his own compulsions (Dostoevsky would agree), and he is *forced* to protest. Unlike Bartleby, who prefers to starve, the hunger artist says, "I couldn't find the food I liked." Kafka's politics here are interior as well as exterior, and the outsider is, within himself, his own meek victim; if it had been possible, he would have surrendered to the world: "I should have made no fuss and stuffed myself like you or anyone else."

In the metaphorical terms I have used, politics enlightens art, art politics. Saroyan's romantic hero of "The Daring Young Man on the Flying Trapeze" (1934) seeks to do both. First, he speaks directly to political matters:

> It was good to be poor, and the Communists—but it was dreadful to be hungry! What appetites they had, how fond they were of food! Empty stomachs. He remembered how greatly he needed food. Every meal was bread and coffee and cigarettes, and now he had no more bread. . . .
>
> If the truth were known, he was half starved, and yet there was still no end of books he ought to read before he died.

This young writer seems to speak of the political so as to point up its separateness from the artistic truth at which Saroyan (and his protagonist) aim: that it is good to die for art, that out of such death comes that state ("dreamless, unalive, perfect") which a mind chained to its body cannot achieve. Perfect art, and the perfect rewards of the artist—"It made him very angry to think that there was no respect for men who wrote"—are available only when human imperfections are removed: in death. Yet this young man is highly political; he and Kafka's hunger artist are in fact quite similar. They are coercing the world to love them by dying away from its nourishment; they are reversing the customary design of power. They are both forced by what is outside their control—the one by economics, the other by absence of provender his body can tolerate—to starve. Yet each is, clearly, fully satisfied only by his death; his dying tells him that his death is what he has wanted, is the only means by which he will achieve what he desires. As Saroyan's writer says, "His life was a private life. He did not wish to destroy this fact. Any other alternative would be better." Of course, the grave's that fine and private place; there are no alternatives.

Knut Hamsun, in *Hunger* (1890), is interested in showing us that his protagonist will starve rather than not write. But he does not want to die. He wants to live *in order to write.* He is inordinately healthy, listening to his interior self, following its demands that he live the life of the writer. But when, as Robert Bly points out in the introduction to his 1967 translation, the interior self tells him to work and live, at the risk of no longer writing, he does so: "The cakes disappeared one after the other. It didn't seem to matter how many I got down. I remained ferociously hungry. Why didn't they help!" Even if this is not the nourishment he should have if the world were perfect, he will eat in order to live in the imperfect world in which artists do not triumph. His subconscious, which has directed his course throughout the novel, tells him that he ought to survive. So he does: he remains in the world and is fed by it, accepts its power over him—"So he gave me a job to do. . . ."—and provides a symbolic opposition to the examples of Kafka's hunger artist and Saroyan's daring young man. Hamsun's writer, perhaps like his author, is a political survivor, an artist who fails; Kafka's and Saroyan's artists, who succeed, cannot survive. Have we, in truth, come so far from the apotheosis of Chatterton? Did the poetry of Plath, Berryman, Sexton threaten us with their deaths because we loved them insufficiently? Were we—the world, the blank wall at which they stared—to be punished by their leaving us? And is that part of the reason for our disproportionate celebration of even their most minor work?

Saroyan uses hunger to make us feel sorry for his protagonist. The weakness of the sentimentality in Saroyan's fiction, particularly in this very important collection, is that Saroyan will do anything to make the reader love his characters. He will demean them, kill them, break their hearts—and not always because the character's inner necessities require such torture; they suffer in order that Saroyan achieve our response. So the young writer starves himself, or enjoys his starvation, because Saroyan believes that the strategy will draw the reader in. Indeed, there is the other motive—to show how the artist flies out beyond mere physicality. But we might want to note that the tactics of literary starvation include a playing on the most sensational, least rational, qualities of the reader.

So Dickens, in *The Old Curiosity Shop*, has Little Nell starving on her journey through the Midlands not only because an industrialized society, and a virulent Quilp, are heartless toward her—although these are part of Dickens' strategy of starvation. His most important motive, one suspects, is to make us feel sorry for Nell: to pull us into his world, and at his mercy, on his terms. Starvation can become a political act on the writer's part, then. He starves his character to assert maximum power over the reader's emotions. We become incapable of rejecting him. He feeds us—*his* idea of nourishment—against our will.

An extension of this idea is the way some writers kill their characters off by violence in order to place us at their mercy. If we disregard the lesser book-club novels, and look at someone like Forster, the point is clearer. Character after character is killed in *The Longest Journey,* and not necessarily because he is doomed by his fate. He dies so that Forster can force his characters to react. Before he knows what to do with Ricky—kill him off, of course—he knocks people down like dominoes, hoping that the deaths will force his characters into focus with what lives remain. While employing the tenderness of the body-count, Forster nevertheless insists on a realistic fiction. His Salisbury Plain writhes with life while his characters are corpses, killed so that his ideas may live. Compare these gratuitous deaths with the coldly rendered, metaphorically functional deaths in *To the Lighthouse.* There it is clear that the novel is about the absence of Mrs. Ramsay, about time: the deaths which an artistic sensibility will try to undo must therefore occur. The reader is not only shocked by the deaths in the Ramsay family, he is saddened. And, as Lily Briscoe tries to reverse time, re-create life through her vision, the reader mourns her failure. Mr. Ramsay springs up from his boat as Gregor Samsa's sister springs to her feet (the butterfly metamorphosing from the pupa which Gregor really was). And because of the deaths, one feels that something basic has been at stake.

Arthur Clennam, in the Marshalsea at the end of *Little Dorrit,* defeated sexually and societally, decides to die; he loses his appetite and his sense of taste, begins to starve and sicken. When Dorritt returns, she lures him back to the world. She reads to him in a voice which evokes Nature's ("At no Mother's knee but hers had he ever dwelt in his youth") and in her voice "are memories of an old feeling of such things": she becomes his mother, the prison cell her womb, he is reborn to the world. Steinbeck effects such a rescue at the end of *The Grapes of Wrath.* Starving, having decided to die—"He said he et, or he wasn't hungry . . ."—the old man is saved by Rose of Sharon. He sups from her nipple, is metaphorically her child. Both are examples of "Caritas Romana," that classical image of charity celebrated in Renaissance, Neoclassical and Romantic art, as the wife, daughter or mother suckling a man who is starving to death in prison. While the sexual implications of the image are immense, one can be equally struck by the fact that the image is so frequently political: the man-as-child is nearly always in jail, a victim of the state.

Roman Charity, a rebellion by brave woman, is political in that the will of the state is defeated. But what if it is the will of that state that we survive, suckle at the breast of government? In that case, the breast, whether proffered by a government or by an earth mother, becomes antagonistic to the self-government of the citizen who wishes to exercise his ultimate will by dying. The modern protagonist slaps the breast aside.*

But Kafka says that he cannot. In Kafka, everything is lost. Even his hunger artist loses the satisfaction of intentionally starving away from the world. Kafka insists on denying to man any franchise whatever: life is what happens to us, not what we do. So even the officer of "In the Penal Colony," who is in charge of the apparatus which engraves onto the prisoner's body with needles and acid the commandment—BE JUST!—which the prisoner is said to have violated, himself becomes a victim of the machine. He elects to leave, in the fashion he chooses, a world he sees as unjust, but he is denied the right. The machine disobeys him: "This was no exquisite torture such as the officer desired, this was plain murder."

"In the Penal Colony" is a political story which contains elements we have found to be central to the modern terror-state. Like "Bartleby," Kafka's story has a figure disenfranchised by political change; instead of (as in the Melville) loss of a Chancery post, or of a job in the Dead Letter Office, we have in the officer a middle-management figure, a Lieutenant Calley who obeys orders. But there is a new Commandant, and the political climate of the penal island has changed. Instead of dedication to the apparatus of tutelary torture, the officer sees a web of intrigue: the new Commandant is influenced by gross sexuality (his laughing ladies) and he is unenthusiastic about the formerly honored torture ritual. The opposition between the Old Commandant and the new, and the importance of the palimpsest of plans for torture, and the prophecy that the buried Old Commandant will

*I am indebted to the fascinating discussion by Robert Rosenblum in his "Caritas Romana after 1760: Some Romantic Lactations," in *Woman as Sex Object, Art News Annual 38,* ed. Thomas B. Hess and Linda Nochlin (New York: Newsweek, Inc., 1972), pp. 43–63.

"rise again and lead his adherents," are all suggestive of an Old Testament world opposed to a New, or anyway an old god seen in opposition to prevailing faith in a new one. If that is so, Kafka politicizes even the heavens.

The point, whether the story is cosmic or earthbound in its implications, is that the dutiful officer is an Eichmann-figure for contemporary readers—not merely because he obeys the Old Commandant's orders with such zeal, no matter their perverted justice and morality, but because his primary concern is *to keep his job*. Like so many middle-management types—think of those Nixon toadies in gray suits and pretty haircuts, sobbing before Senator Ervin that they cooperated with the rudiments of a police state to "stay part of the team," or "because it was my job to obey Mr. Haldeman"—the officer's central allegiance is less to the beloved Old Commandant than to the machine of torture and its tending: "I can no longer reckon on any further extension of the method, it takes all my energy to maintain it as it is." One recalls Gregor's fear that he will lose the job he hates—or Kafka's same worry.

The job is to process victims for the sake of the process itself. The victims, of course, receive no justice as they are tortured to "BE JUST!" They are paradigms of the terror-state's victims (and of humankind in the terrifying cosmos in which such states thrive). It is important, then, that they be fed. The officer explains the apparatus:

> Here, into this electrically heated basin at the head of the bed, some warm rice pap is poured, from which the man, if he feels like it, can take as much as his tongue can lap. Not one of them ever misses the chance. I can remember none, and my experience is extensive. Only about the sixth hour does the man lose all desire to eat. I usually kneel down here at that moment and observe what happens. The man rarely swallows his last mouthful, he only rolls it around his mouth and spits it out into the pit.

The officer's happy description is that of the man who knows and loves the intricacy of his work. It is not difficult (though it is awful) to imagine Eichmann explaining that they are sorted here, the sick are lined up here, their clothes are dropped off here, and here is where I stand to watch them.

"Not one of them ever misses the chance," says Kafka's officer: the breast is not pawed aside, and the world forces itself down the throats of the condemned. The sixth hour is generally the moment just before death for the prisoner. He does not rebel when he spits the food out, he is considered enlightened (and ready for burial); he goes to his death with a mouth encrusted by what the world would feed him. Self-determination dies with him.

It is that kind of death-in-life, inflicted by others, which Beckett's Molloy fights off. When Lousse requires of Molloy that he live with her, and forces food upon him—"the substances she insinuated thus into my various systems"—she makes him her replacement for the dog she says he's killed. He is punished by feeding, reduced, as Thoreau says he is, in "Civil Disobedience," by the minions of the state who "had resolved to punish my body; just as boys, if they cannot come at some person against whom they have a spite, will abuse his dog." Thoreau in jail looks out "through an iron grating which strained the light." Molloy, in Lousse's imprisoning house, looks out through a window on a moon strained by its bars so that "two bars divided it in three segments, of which the middle remained constant, while little by little the right gained what the left lost." Each writer makes the moon—one of the world's facts—a function of his imagination. So too does he make the imprisoning world itself, and its attempts to nourish him with its facts against his will, functions of his imagination. And through the imagination each escapes, by refusal, or in Thoreau's case postulation of refusal, of what the world would serve for dinner.

Young women do so daily, by retreating into the psychic agonies of *anorexia nervosa:* they find that they cannot eat, they vomit up their food, are skeletons, sometimes die. The women who withdraw their appetites look sexless, finally, like the wide-eyed young Kafka—whose photographs put one in mind of staring emaciated concentration-camp survivors.

A woman who retreats is Gail Godwin's protagonist in "A Sorrowful Woman." "*Once upon a time there was a wife and mother one too many times,*" the story begins, and by the end she is sealed away in a house-keeper's room, unable to cope (and unwilling to cope) with husband or son. She becomes "a young queen, a virgin in a tower," and her rebellion is analogous to Gregor Samsa's, and to Bartleby's as well; in her room stocked with cigarettes, books, bread and cheese, she "didn't need much." She eventually prepares to die by baking bread, roasting a turkey and a ham, making three pies, custards; she does two weeks' laundry, makes drawings for her son, writes love sonnets to her husband. In other words, she performs all the chores—symbolic actions as well—the world (according to Godwin) expects of a wife and mother. Another reading, of course, is that she does so not out of love, or guilt, but that she leaves behind mementos of what killed her. Her metaphorical suicide message, then, is one of harsh accusation: *look what your expectations have done to me.* The husband discovers her corpse and simultaneously the son asks, "Can we eat the turkey for supper?" She is their meat. She refuses to be nourished in their world; it is they who devour her. She partially resembles Kafka's hunger artist, and her family—the world—are like the young panther in the dead artist's cage: "the joy of life streamed with such ardent passion from his throat that for the onlookers it was not easy to stand the shock of it. . . ." But they "did not want ever to move away."

Such withdrawals are often central to recent fiction by women, for the women in these works are, foremost, victims. There is currently a premium on female victimization, and publishers, riding the commercial crest, see to it that we have an overabundance. Although the focus is new, though not so new as the press agents and book reviewers tell us, we need think only of Prufrock, Leopold Bloom, Lady Brett, Caddy Compson, to remember that all of our significant modern protagonists are somehow imprisoned. And we need think only of Eudora Welty's Jack Renfro and Julia Mortimer to remember that our fiction is not without heroic figures.

But we recall our heroes infrequently. For each Rosacoke or Milo Mustian, Artur Sammler, Invisible Man, we can—and do—name a hundred protagonists who are destroyed by the world. The likes of Lowry's Geoffrey Firmin have given the hero a bad name: we call him dead. He isn't, but he must, it seems, die to triumph in contemporary writing.

For when our heroes do succeed, it is in the dark heart. We see them in the agonies of a defeat and epiphany which we tend to accept as metaphoric of our own self-consuming enlightenments. They win by living *within.* Their emblem is the maggot of hope which writhes in the age's excrement.

Examining the hero in terms of the world—the pressure of too many frightened people, the force of institutional events, the daily diminution—we turn back to Kafka, who says that one may not refuse by means of muscle, courage, the imagination. His hunger artist *must* starve, the officer's dying prisoners have to lap at the teat they're strapped to. According to Kafka, that we insist on accepting the world's nourishment, no matter how much we desire to forsake it, is the tragedy of our entrapment. It is the reason such wise political parabolists as Gandhi, Sakharov, Dick Gregory, Cesar Chavez, South African protesters like Mandela, have insisted on showing us that they starve on our behalf. They are sometimes, now, these starvers, a prick to our conscience. When they die, we may call them heroes. And so it is with our literary heroes. They do not win on our behalf unless they achieve mortality. When we write our most prayerful art, the hero, in opposition to his nineteenth-century predecessor, survives. When we write this age's interior realism, the hero survives only metaphorically, by choosing to die in his skin rather than with thousands in a furnace, or a mass grave.

◄§ *(WE ARE DEAD NOW)* §►

MITHRA, SATURN, fairies and witches, Druids with cruel knives, the Celtic goddess Strenia, Mari Lwyd of Wales, and the Lord of Misrule: the year is haunted, as our lives are, by powerful spirits. They lurk in the forest and loom from the garden post, or the timbers of an old house, or the branches of a Christmas tree. Dickens smelled these spirits' presence in the psychic air as one might smell the imminence of snow. In *A Christmas Carol* he responded to such hauntings and added some of his own—Ebenezer Scrooge, Tiny Tim Cratchit, the faceless Ghost of Christmas Yet to Come. He also confessed, in the *Carol* and in other stories celebrating the death and renewal of the year, his own renewal and death.

We need to remind ourselves, as Dickens so frequently did, that when he was about twelve, therefore probably in 1824, his father John Dickens, a minor functionary in the Navy's pay office, and like his wife a hopeless profligate, was sent to the Marshalsea debtor's prison in London. Charles, earlier removed from school (which he had loved), was sent to work in Warren's Blacking factory, 30, Strand, where with boys he thought low and in conditions that were surely both unhealthy and unhappy he pasted labels on bottles of black goo.

Prisoners in the Marshalsea could live with their families while awaiting the miraculous arrival of money that would pay their debts and secure their release. (Of course, while the families could come and go, the prisoners could not leave to work to earn their freedom; a convenient and wealthy death in the family was therefore a prisoner's best hope.) The Dickens family moved in with the father, but the boy lived alone, in a furnished room, seeing his family only after work and at breakfast. He felt threatened by his long walk to and from work through neighborhoods that were unsavory; he felt threatened by his parents' abandonment; he felt threatened by what he had become: the bright boy who had lived with books had only recently been forced to pawn them. He felt, finally, powerless. He was a small, shamed scrap of person in the huge, noisy, cruel and stinking city. He never forgot. As a grown man, he could not pass Warren's Blacking without weeping at the smell. He never told his wife and children of his two- or three-month exile. We know of it only because he wrote an Autobiographical Fragment for his friend and first biographer, John Forster.

And Dickens memorialized his sense of terrified smallness by holding his horror to his breast throughout his life and by developing his talent for seeing double. A great measure of his achievement must be attributed to his ability to simultaneously portray the adult's view of the world and the child's—especially the child's feeling of insecurity, of nightmare terror, of smallness in the dangerous large world. Thus Dickens' affection for undersized children as characters who are crippled or bullied or starved. Thus his insistence on writing of children who were not merely miniature adults but people in their own right—and people who, furthermore, so often had to force themselves to behave like adults while feeling like little more than babies (Nell of *The Old Curiosity Shop,* Florence of *Dombey and Son*); the pain of such necessity is never absent from Dickens' novels. So *Great Expectations* (1864) begins with an orphan at his family's grave, a "small bundle of shivers growing afraid of it all and beginning to cry." So *Oliver Twist* (which appeared serially in 1837–39) begins with the newborn Oliver as an "item of mortality."

And so we have *A Christmas Carol,* written about an old man by one relatively young (Dickens was thirty-one when it was published), complete with a sympathetic dying child who is crippled. Dickens was fond of permitting himself to be forced, by the demands of his readers, and therefore large sales, as well as by his stories' intrinsic needs, to kill off in dream and in narrative fact such attractive young characters as Meg in *The Chimes,* and Little Nell, Paul Dombey, and of course Tiny Tim. Remember Dickens' feelings of helplessness as he described them in his Autobiographical Fragment, and as he echoed the Fragment in the very autobiographical *David Copperfield:*

> I was not beaten, or starved; but the wrong that was done to me had no intervals of relenting, and was done in a systematic, passionless manner. Day after day, week after week, month after

month, I was coldly neglected. I wonder sometimes, when I think of it, what they would have done if I had been taken with an illness; whether I should have lain down in my lonely room, and languished through it in my usual solitary way, or whether anybody would have helped me out.

Contemplating a languishing death, becoming ill or deformed, maimed or merely febrile—like so many of his young characters—Dickens, in book after book, rehearsed his own tragedy. And in the mind of a fictive child, himself, using his fictive children, he threatened the world of adults with his own sad death.

He never forgot. He continued all his life to rally to the small and wronged, to rage with his famous angers at their plight and those who caused it, and thereby was able to commemorate his own injuries, serve his own needs. Like his simultaneous vision of child and adult, his generosities were simultaneous—public and inward. And he was never more double, more selfish and generous, than when he wrote his Christmas books. They were meant to cheer the reader, to attack the wrong and bolster the right, and to turn a handsome profit. Beginning in 1843, he published (in order) *A Christmas Carol, The Chimes, The Cricket on the Hearth, The Battle of Life,* and *The Haunted Man.* Dickens became engulfed by the winter of 1849 in the writing of *David Copperfield.* Although he offered a Christmas story each year in his journal, *Household Words,* he didn't write another Christmas book.

The end of the series coincides with Dickens' dark descent into his own memories, as he begins *Copperfield. The Haunted Man,* at this point of his writing life just completed, contains this passage: "Then, as Christmas is a time in which, of all times in the year, the memory of every remediable sorrow, wrong, and trouble in the world around us, should be active with us. . . ." At Christmastime, and surely in his Christmas books, Dickens had his Christmas cake and ate it too. While he can have Scrooge's nephew say that it is "a good time: a kind, forgiving, charitable, pleasant time," he can also think those bleak thoughts of "every remediable sorrow, wrong, and trouble." In other words, Christmas to Dickens is *not* only the commemoration of home, hearth, cheer and generosity; it is the time when one entertains another Dickensian double vision: the recollection, in sore detail, of each cruelty perpetrated upon one, and then the forgiveness of those who have done the harm. It is a way of being Christian and wrathful at once, vindictive and forgiving at once, tearful and smiling at once. Janus, the two-faced god, was celebrated by ancient Romans hard upon the Saturnalia, from which we derive customs for the celebration of Christmas.

So we are in 1843, and Charles Dickens, the successful author of *Sketches by Boz, The Posthumous Papers of the Pickwick Club, Oliver Twist, The Life and Adventures of Nicholas Nickleby* and *Barnaby Rudge,* is issuing in monthly numbers *The Life and Adventures of Martin Chuzzlewit.* It is not going well, and the sales figures prove it. Dickens, perhaps unusually distractible at this time, notes an appeal in the *Times* for the Ragged Schools; interested in such a system of charitable education of paupers and mindful of a recently published report on child employment, Dickens is thinking about some kind of article on the children of the poor. At the urging of his patron, Miss Coutts, he visits a ragged school in Saffron Lane, and he is horrified and touched by the plight of the neglected children. His distaste and anger percolate while he works at *Chuzzlewit.* And then, a few weeks later, he goes with his sister Fanny to speak at the Manchester Athenaeum, a workingman's institute; his topic is the combating of poverty through education. While speaking, he thinks of using aspects of his cause in fiction, not in an article. So, burning with anger, wanting to translate it into language, perhaps motivated by his need for money and the slumping sales of *Chuzzlewit,* Dickens, by mid-October, is at work on *A Christmas Carol,* a story built around the structure of a Christmas song. And though he has complaints about his publisher's distribution and advertising of the book, Dickens has every right to be pleased when it comes out. The critical reception, though mixed, is good enough. The sales are large. Available by December 19, it sells out its first edition of six thousand copies at once. By March 1844, *A Christmas Carol* is in its sixth edition.

On December 26, 1843, Dickens, Forster and other friends, Jane Welsh Carlyle among them, attended a birthday party at the home of the eminent actor Macready. In her letter to Miss Coutts, Jane Carlyle captures not only Dickens' celebration of his own success, but his sense of Christmas rejoicing:

> Dickens and Forster above all exerted themselves till the perspiration was pouring down and they seemed *drunk* with their efforts! Only think of that excellent Dickens playing the *conjuror* for one

whole hour—the *best* conjuror I ever saw. . . . This part of the entertainment concluded with a plum pudding made out of raw flour, raw eggs,—all the usual raw ingredients—boiled in a gentleman's hat—and tumbled out reeking—all in one minute before the eyes of the astonished children and astonished grown people! that trick—and his other of changing ladies' pocket handkerchiefs into comfits—and a box full of bran into a box full of a—live guinea pig!—would enable him to make a handsome subsistence let the bookseller trade go as it please—!

Dickens is the magical spirit itself; he is the ghost of plenty, the nephew of Scrooge, and the cheerful cry of Tiny Tim, and all at once. It is worth remembering him this way, because the passage to such gaiety, as *A Christmas Carol* shows us, is a dark one.

Dickens' feelings of intimacy with his audience have been growing. (They will grow to such an extent that, when he separates from his wife, Katherine, he addresses the issue in the columns of his *Household Words*.) Here, in what is subtitled "A Ghost Story of Christmas," Dickens speaks of Scrooge being as near to a ghostly figure "as I am now to you, and I am standing in spirit at your elbow." Dickens loves his readers, and he wishes to be loved by them in turn. But he also *is* that ghostly figure. He wishes to sweetly haunt—"to raise the Ghost of an Idea," as he puns in his preface. He is not only acting the benefactor of his audience and recalling the child who loved his nurse's frightening stories of Captain Murderer (who baked his wives in pies and ate them); he is reflecting the actualities of Christmas myth, in which fertility spirits, and the returning souls of the dead, have always played a part. We are to experience the story of Ebenezer Scrooge, a man who is dead because his soul is crushed. Thanks to Christmas, he will be reborn. But Scrooge, and not Marley, is the very first ghost we meet.

Scrooge is described as a winter spirit, a child's notion of a goblin, as much as he is a man—"squeezing, wrenching, grasping, scraping, clutching"—and we are told that he "carried his own low temperature always about with him." He is the essence of chill. When his nephew calls upon him, the young man is "all in a glow" and his face is "ruddy," his breath smoking; he is the essence of warmth, and we see that we not only read a tale of human feelings but an allegory, a contest of basic forces. Within moments, Scrooge has denied heat to his poor clerk, complained about the necessity for giving him the day off at

Christmas, and turned down a request that he aid the poor. He is cold and dead of heart. But we might wish to remember too that his repartee with his nephew, about the "keeping" of Christmas, is witty and theatrical, and that his cruel refusal to assist the poor is as bright as Scrooge is bleak—which is to say that he is not only a caricature of greed but a *character,* for whom it is possible for the reader to entertain a few scraps of admiration.

Dickens is never only a teacher or only a Jeremiah. He is a great artist, and his artistry shows itself at once. In describing the offices of Scrooge & Marley, he works like an Impressionist painter, offering candle flares on a dark wintry day that are "like ruddy smears upon the palpable brown air." And in doing more than crying *Ghost!* when Marley appears, doing more than labeling the supernatural, Dickens works to make the spectral display mundane characteristics. That is what frightens people about ghosts—not that they're called ghosts, and not that they're dead, but that they're *here,* in our world, out of place. So when Marley comes, his hair is "curiously stirred, as if by breath or hot-air." The intimation of Hell's heat is satisfactory; the fact that we attend to corporeal physical facts, on a purportedly disembodied spirit, is masterful. So too is Marley's binding of his head before he departs from Scrooge, who records "the smart sound its teeth made, when the jaws were brought together by the bandage": the resonant particularity of that *click!,* the verisimilitude of solid teeth in a creature of air, is a sign of Dickens' genius.

When the first of the three Christmas spirits appears, Scrooge has fallen asleep. Wakened by the tolling of the hour, Scrooge says that it isn't possible for him to have slept so long. Time, he thinks, has run backward, or else he has lost a day. "It isn't possible," he says, "that anything has happened to the sun, and this is twelve at noon!" The point for us is that what we might call actual time has been shattered. Dickens, henceforth, in each of the staves representing visitations of the Spirits of Christmas, will deal not with the world's time, but with interior time. The dreamworld here extends the boundaries of Dickens' fiction and of fiction in general. Dickens knows that within the mind, especially the mind under great stress—that of Sikes the murderer in *Oliver Twist,* that of Jonas Chuzzlewit, another murderer— boundaries of space and time are meaningless, and the tortured interior self lives by other rules and in other dimensions. This use of the inner world, the fictive expansion of which made Dickens' fiction grow, and therefore that of writers as disparate as Kafka and Joyce, is here a signal accomplishment. His Scrooge, while cruel and pained and extreme, is no murderer; Dickens can stop short of those who are ultimately alienated through crime and violence as he operates in the midnight world of his characters. Hereafter he will be able to give us the arrested Miss Havisham of *Great Expectations,* the eternally immature Skimpole of *Bleak House.*

Shortly after he acknowledges Marley's ghost, Scrooge says to him that "you may be an undigested bit of beef, a blot of mustard. . . ." While fearing what he thinks of as a spirit, Scrooge, "not much in the habit of cracking jokes," nevertheless engages in repartee. He is working at "keeping down his own terror." He is, in other words, both witty and brave. We are given another signal that he might possibly be a man worth reclaiming—might justify all the efforts being made to assure his rebirth. Thus, in the third stave, when the second of the spirits appears, Scrooge is described as keeping a weather eye for its entrance: "For he wished to challenge the Spirit on the moment of its appearance, and did not wish to be taken by surprise and made nervous." He is both resolute and adamant in his nearsightedness, but he is also, like Dickens, doing his best to be uncontrolled by a situation that does control him; there *is* something admirable about him. And he is capable of learning. By the time the last spirit has arrived, Scrooge cries that the "night is waning," and the time is "precious" to him. He is counting interior hours, like sacred beads, and he knows that he needs to be saved and that there is little time left for his soul. Furthermore, with the final spirit, he offers no quips, no badinage; he has at last learned, and he says, "I know your purpose is to do me good, and as I hope to live to be another man from what I was, I am prepared to bear you company, and do it with a thankful heart." Whereas he could not accept the gifts of good wishes from his nephew in the tale's opening pages, because he feared that they signified a spiritual transaction he could not afford, he now acknowledges that he *can* receive—in this case, wisdom. And he signals that fact by offering none of the aggressive humor with which he has heretofore greeted either warm emotion in general, or the story's ghosts in particular.

In almost the numerical center of the *Carol,* and surely at its spiritual core, is the dreamy visitation with the first Spirit of Christmas, that of Christmas Past, to the time of young Scrooge. In the only childhood scene involving Scrooge, Dickens attempts to offer a dra-

matic cause for such behavior as the grown man displays. We see the
boy sent away from home, now alone at school "when all the other
boys" have been allowed "home for the jolly holidays." So the boy who
was taken out of school, and the boy who was exiled from his family,
remembers—in the spirit of recollection and *then* forgiveness—both
exile and the school of which he felt deprived. Scrooge's beloved sister
is named Fan, just as Dickens' own sister is named Fanny. Fan tells
Scrooge that he is to be brought home by her, and "You're to be a
man!" she says, "and are never to come back here."

One can now weigh Dickens' psychic investment in the *Carol.* His
own childhood plight, the source of such continuing agony to him, is
revisited—in the persona of Scrooge. It permits Dickens, in the fantasy contained in his fiction, to utter a prayer—spoken on behalf of the
young Scrooge, and also on his own. So many of his wishes for children must have actually been spoken not only on their behalf, but on
behalf of the small boy Dickens, arrested, in perpetual pain, in the
dark places of Dickens' mind, brought out again and again in those
dream scenes enacted in his imagination, where time and space were
shaped by the inner vision. Dickens' prayer is that he may no longer be
an exile, may feel the richness of what he believes a family's love ought
to be. The peculiar line, "And you're to be a man!" spoken as if a father's wishes that a child return can confer maturity, is resonant in this
passage. Surely, one can infer that manhood means independence to
Dickens. The awarding of that station does not mean only that the boy
may wear trousers or feel that he is respectable. It means independence from manipulation by elders; it means that one is admitted to
the family once more, and then is in a position to declare one's independence of certain of its arbitrarinesses.

Note, from the Autobiographical Fragment, the syntax of Dickens'
confession, which so echoes that of his fiction: "I often forget in my
dreams that I have a dear wife and children; even that I am a man...."
In each case, as Dickens writes, he *is* a man. One senses that he does
not always believe in his own safety, his own distance, from his childhood's vulnerabilities. One senses Dickens' feeling that the nightmare
of his boyhood abandonment, and his resultant unforgiving anger, always threaten to draw him back. And one is tempted to ask why Dickens chose to show Scrooge's unhappy and alienated childhood, except
to offer it as a cause—*the* cause?—for the wounded state in which we
find him, unable to give or receive love. A possible answer, of course,

is that Dickens, whose portrait of Scrooge at points suggests Dickens' own inner portrait, fears that Scrooge's fate might be his own, and that this powerful and cautionary haunting is aimed at himself as well as at his readers. The result is that this heartfelt Christmas book is the greatest of the five, and the most enduring.

If Scrooge might be considered, loosely, to be something of a minor Macbeth, then the three characters, gathered in a London slum in the final stave, surely belong with him. Dickens is at his best here, relishing his description of the nasty elements of a London he knew and had feared. Two women with bundles join an old man, and together they cackle: they are the three witches from *Macbeth*, instructing and prophesying through a dream—Scrooge's spirit-induced vision. They have robbed dead Scrooge, who now lies as just an "item of mortality" on a lonely bed. A dreadful forecast of his death is shown to Scrooge, and his ultimate aloneness seems inescapable. So is his virtual destruction. As dogs run with the bones of the dead in an overcrowded Victorian graveyard, so these creatures carry Scrooge's buttons, a brooch, a pencil case, a shirt, bed-curtains, a blanket. Scrooge, who lived by things, is now reduced to things, himself "a something covered up, which, although it was dumb, announced itself in awful language."

And, emerging from that terrible vision and from his soul's long night, Scrooge cries, "I don't know what day of the month it is!" for he is "quite a baby." He has been born anew. Real isolation, for Dickens, is death. All of his murderers and the cruelest of his other characters suffer isolation, if not physical death, in repayment for their trespasses. But Scrooge is spared because he has learned. Reborn, he becomes the Pickwick figure, the loving (and rich) uncle who so often, in Dickens' novels, appears to assure a bright hearthside, long life and ready cash. He provides a turkey, he raises Cratchit's pay, and he stands by to provide what is necessary to see to Tim's health. This is a tale of and for the middle class (not those paupers who might have excited its first imaginings), and money is one of the household gods. Used selfishly and worshipped with cravenness, money turns on its supplicant like a sour-tempered snake, Dickens seems to say. Used well, and then in good quantities, money blesses its possessors. It is always a major character in Dickens' fiction.

Tiny Tim "did NOT die," we are told at the end of the *Carol*. But Dickens, the boy shut out of the world he craved—school, books, family, security, what might in general be expected by a child of his talent and wit—Dickens himself may have died a metaphorical death. His subsequent work suggests the possibility.

He continued his tradition of telling Christmas stories to his readers, and he wrote and published in his *Household Words* for December 21, 1850 (the Christmas number), a familiar essay called "A Christmas Tree," which he chose for the volume *Reprinted Pieces* (1858).

It is really a short story, and it is a hymn to memory as well as Christmas. The narrator has gone on a Christmas visit and has watched children become enchanted by the toys and ornaments on their tree. Back home, "alone, the only person in the house awake," he recalls a more metaphorical than actual tree, "by which we climbed to real life." (Prince Albert brought the German Christmas tree to widespread use in England in 1841; it's not likely that Dickens had a tree as a boy; and neither Bob Cratchit nor Fred, Scrooge's nephew, has a tree.) On the fictive tree, then, as he did on his fictive carol's staves, Dickens locates his simultaneities of Christmas—past and present, terror and delight, domestic affection and cold alienation, maturity and childhood—and they are experienced at once.

So while he celebrates the toys of childhood, Dickens also sees them as "an immense array of shapeless things," which causes him to remember not pleasure but a Scrooge-like loss of time: he recalls "being sent early to bed, as a punishment for some small offence, and waking in two hours, with a sensation of having been asleep two nights . . . and the oppression of a weight of remorse."

Searching amid the branches, in memory, on his metaphorical tree, the narrator finds not only innocent pleasures but reminders, emblems, of his inner darknesses. A toy circus tumbler leers with "lobster eyes" and the boy "affected to laugh very much, but in my heart of hearts was extremely doubtful of him." There is a jack-in-the-box that is "demoniacal" and inescapable, appearing thereafter in the boy's dreams. A cardboard man, hung on the wall and pulled by a string, is "sinister." And recollections of these frights occur amid references to Dickens' own favorite boyhood reading: the *Arabian Nights' Entertainments,* "Mother Bunch's Wonders," which included tales of Robin Hood, the Yellow Dwarf and Valentine, and both *Robinson Crusoe* and *The Adventures of Philip Quarll.* So Dickens is basing his story on his own childhood, one might reasonably hypothesize.

And the key to his need to confront ghosts and the worst within mundane man, while at his Christmas play, might be found in Dickens' boyhood too. In his "Christmas Tree" frivolities, Dickens describes a doll with an immovable mask. He acknowledges that it was not hideous, "is even meant to be droll," and that "I was not afraid of *her*." But he asks, "When did that dreadful Mask first look at me? Who put it on, and why was I so frightened that the sight of it is an era in my life?"

Christmas brings our narrator face to face with a terrifying effigy, the cause of nightmares—the boy awakens, covered with sweat, screaming, "O I know it's coming! O the mask!" Like Dickens, and here speaking for him, the narrator of "A Christmas Tree" is sent by Christmas sentiment back to boyhood joys which he reveals to have been boyhood nightmares too. The doll is lifelike, but is also, in its stillness, like death. One can become used to such a simultaneous, yet opposed, set of characteristics, as one can become used to a great deal. But then a mask, part of the doll but also an intentional screening-off of what has become customary, is introduced. The child experiences a frustration of what is customary or familiar, and the result is fright and anger. The usual world has been taken away—as it was when Scrooge was taken from home, or when Dickens was—and the world becomes a new and difficult, if not outright terrifying, place.

But Christmas is a time not only for remembering, Dickens has told us, but for forgiving. So the nominally Christian Dickens quotes, in "A Christmas Tree," "Forgive them, for they know not what they do." The child in this narrative, and the child in Scrooge's story—the child in Dickens as well?—has been exiled, crucified. But as Scrooge in his fantasy was allowed home, so is this narrator: "And I *do* come home at Christmas. We all do, or we all should. We all come home, or ought to come home, for a short holiday—the longer, the better—from the great boarding-school, where we are for ever working at our arithmetical slates, to take, and give a rest."

The narrator is Dickens, as Dickens was Scrooge: sent away from home to be "for ever working at . . . arithmetical slates," getting and spending, and getting on, and growing rich, and being famous. But he is always exiled, always walled away from what was usual—or, in sad memory, rendered usual—and always at Christmas time he recollects what he had, or wished to have, as a paradise that is lost.

The narrator of "A Christmas Tree" turns it into another "Ghost Story of Christmas"—a convention of the holiday and surely one for Dickens. He introduces well-wrought but usual gothic stories, then makes himself a ghost: "We said so, before we died (we are dead now)," he says. He haunts the Christmas of the story as other supernatural beings haunt other Christmases. And he concludes the story with Luke: "This, in remembrance of Me." He offers the fiction as a transubstantiative gift.

If those words imply that the narrator, or Dickens, has climbed the metaphorical tree to such heroic and cruciform heights—that Dickens, by virtue of his early suffering, is in his memory to die again and once again be born each Christmas—then it is possible that the pages of his Christmas writings do reveal why the artist who created so much life was drawn to tell us of himself, and in a coffinlike parenthesis, that "(we are dead now)."

Because Edmund Wilson paid attention so well, it was he who saw in Henry Dickens' *Memories of My Father* at least some of the importance of the following scene. Henry recalled that his father was drawing closer to death in 1859 when at a party the family played a word-association game. Charles Dickens' turn came around, and he said only, "Warren's Blacking, 30, Strand." His voice was peculiar. No one understood the meaning of his words. The fire was high. Dickens rested on a sofa while about him the family made merry. And of course it was a party for Christmas.

✍ *HOLMES'S OCCUPATION* ❧

HOLMES WASN'T only a snoop, he was a literary character. Dr. Watson wasn't only a man of medicine, but a writer as well. And though they were celebrated by readers of the day for different reasons— large, heroic, sometimes silly ones—and though we seek out Holmes and Watson, still, because of their daring, acumen and size, we might look to them too because sometimes we can see Sherlock Holmes being written in front of our eyes.

Mr. Sherlock Holmes, by firing shots from his pistol, had carved the initials VR, for *Victoria Regina,* on the wall of 221B Baker Street, London. It was 1887, and for £25 a manuscript of a story about Holmes, after several rejections, was sold to a publisher who performed the signal service of bringing out *A Study in Scarlet,* in which a character who thereafter disappears forever makes a historic introduction: "Dr. Watson, Mr. Sherlock Holmes."

For Holmes and Watson, born in stories, stepped out of them. Like Falstaff, Holmes and Watson survived, and thrived outside, the fictive context that had first given them life; they are referred to and are recognized as people, not as characters. By 1893 Doyle, their creator, came to tire of writing Holmes stories and decided to kill his hero off in "The Final Problem," plunging him down into the Reichenbach Falls as he struggled in the grasp of his archfoe, the evil genius Dr. Moriarty. The world reacted to this death with horror and shock, and not as if a literary creation had disappeared. Men in London wore mourning weeds, and Doyle received letters of protest and sorrow, begging him to return Holmes to life. One devastated reader began her entreaty with this salutation: "You Brute."

While Holmes continued to appear in stories, Arthur Conan Doyle received letters addressed to the detective, in which help was sought in the solution of knotty problems. A press-clipping bureau wrote to Watson, in care of Doyle, asking whether Mr. Holmes might not wish to subscribe to their service. When Holmes more or less retired, Doyle reports in his *Memories and Adventures,* a number of elderly women wrote offering to keep house for Holmes.

Arthur Conan Doyle's own struggles as a doctor in a failing medical practice, and later as a spiritualist who wished to be remembered for achievements other than Holmes, have also become part of literary folklore. Few readers don't recall a small something of the journey of Mr. Doyle (later Sir Arthur), the unsuccessful physician of Southsea, Hampshire, who published two detective novels, the 1887 *A Study in Scarlet,* and the 1890 *The Sign of the Four,* who studied in Vienna to become an eye specialist, and then was a medical failure in Montague Street, London, and who, to pay his bills, returned to Sherlock Holmes by publishing "A Scandal in Bohemia" in the *Strand Magazine* in 1891. When Doyle killed Holmes, who affected him like *pâté de foie gras*—"of which I once ate so much, so that the name of it gives me a sickly feeling to this day"—he almost stuck to his resolve. But money, that great motivator of writers, brought Holmes back: *Strand* offered Doyle £100 for every one thousand words about Holmes that he might deliver, and *Collier's* chimed in with an offer of $5000 for a Holmes story. Doyle gave in.

If Holmes was almost not reborn, he was also almost not born in the first place. He makes his first appearance in *A Study in Scarlet,* and is customarily traced to one Sherringford Holmes of an early Doyle manuscript, who resided at 221B Upper Baker Street with an Ormond Sacker recently back from Afghanistan. But Doyle's son, Adrian Conan Doyle, celebrating his father in what Holmes might call a "small study" or "trifling monograph," tells us this:

> In rummaging through one of my father's old chests, I unearthed a bundle of his early medical treatises and, tucked among them, a collection of five manuscripts in his writing. They prove that Dr. Watson not only came to life before Holmes, but that the original *Study in Scarlet* had no Sherlock Holmes in it! Watson alone held the stage. . . . The title of *A Study in Scarlet* has been roughly scratched out in this original MS., which takes the form of a lengthy dramatic script, and altered to *The Angels of Darkness.*

While it in no way detracts from Holmes, this discovery does
confer a new and pleasing distinction upon Watson.

Watson was, and still is for us, Holmes's Sancho Panza, as well as—in
Holmes's own words—his Boswell. For Arthur Conan Doyle, Watson
was an embodiment of some of himself. And for us, Watson, with his
bluff English exclamations and his heartfelt concern for what is ordinary and right, is the way we reach and are reached by the colder and
more distant Holmes.

In the tedious and ill-shaped *Study in Scarlet*, we are not only introduced to Watson and Holmes, but to the pattern of their fictive behavior, which is pretty much established in 1887 for the fifty-six short
stories that will follow. First Watson refers to the recent Holmes-
Watson history. Then, once Holmes is discussed, Watson—the author
who publishes his tales of Holmes—will apologize for resorting to
sneaky authorial tricks in order to glorify his friend. And then we get
an example, despite those apologies, of just how godlike Holmes
can be.

So in *Scarlet* we meet a Holmes who has just recently finished flail-
ing away with a stick at bodies in the dissecting room of a medical college, in order to study bruising after death. He reports, immodestly
enough but no doubt with accuracy, that he has just perfected "the
most practical medico-legal discovery for years . . . an infallible test
for blood stains." He impresses Watson by telling him, "You have been
in Afghanistan, I perceive"; he agrees to share cheap quarters with
Watson at 221B Baker Street, if Watson doesn't mind Holmes's strong
pipe tobacco, his being "down in the dumps" sometimes, and his playing of the violin. In a very few pages, then, we encounter the seeds
of the detective's historic idiosyncracies—including the cocaine in-
jections to which Holmes must resort when his mind cannot find
stimulation in the activity of the criminals he opposes: the "dumps"
into which he declines when there isn't work for him to do. We also get,
in the next few pages of *A Study in Scarlet*, a disquisition on the Science of Deduction (as Holmes calls it), and Watson's famous chart of
Holmes's limits; they include his ignorance of literature, which Holmes
again and again disproves in later stories, and his failure to know—he
says that in his trade it is useless to know—that the earth revolves
around the sun.

The pattern of *Scarlet*, containing the pattern of the stories, continues. A visitor or message arrives; it may be a client, a policeman in need of advice, a cable or a letter. Holmes and Watson are required to make a journey, to hear a tale of woe. Sherlock Holmes acts powerfully and with secrecy. The action is resolved, and Holmes explains what he did. In addition, we have in the stories Watson's early references to those tantalizing and never-told stories of other cases: the story of the Giant Rat of Sumatra "for which the world is not prepared"; the affair of the Boulevard assassin; the adventure of the Paradol Chamber; the "shocking affair of the Dutch steamship *Friesland,* which nearly cost us both our lives"; the curious affair of the aluminum crutch; the strange business of the red leech.

The stories, though fashioned according to a simple and repeated pattern by Doyle, continue to hold sway over their readers. Part of their success, surely, is verisimilitude. They have a shared history (those cases for which the world is not prepared), which after a while takes on a feeling of actuality. They have quarters that we come to think of as real; it is as if two great boys shared digs in which one practiced pistol marksmanship on the walls, injected cocaine, scraped at a violin balanced across his knee, while the other—his counterweight— was neat, bourgeois, and something of a writer. We can see the tantalus, the seltzer-making gasogene, the door through which Mrs. Hudson fetches meals at odd hours and escorts women in distress and noblemen perplexed by a changing world.

We're persuaded of the genuineness of these characters because of the hundreds of specific references to the furnishings and apparatus of their ordinary days and extraordinary sallies forth—Watson's pistol, for example, and Holmes's stout stick. (The deerstalker hat, as famous as Holmes himself, was not supplied by Doyle but by the magazine illustrator, Sidney Paget. He used his brother Walter as a model for his sketches; whereas Doyle intended Holmes as ugly, Paget made him as handsome as Walter was.) We come to rely upon seeing the usual details, as we do with any eccentric we enjoy and wish to remark upon. Repetition, then, and detail—the heart of Holmes.

Part of that heart, though, must be laid to Doyle's admiration for Holmes. It is not only that Doyle modeled Holmes on a teacher he much admired, Joseph Bell, thinking, as Doyle says he did, "of his eagle face, of his curious ways, of his eerie trick of spotting details." Doyle goes on: "If he were a detective, he would surely have reduced this fascinating but unorganized business to something nearer an exact science." Clearly, Doyle admired Holmes the scientist. But, equally clearly, he admired in him a fellow adventurer: Doyle hunted whales, voyaged to West Africa, went to Egypt and South Africa, fought political battles and endured hazards at the British front in the Great War; Holmes went among the lowlife of London, fought great bruisers hand to hand, and went alone on the Devon moors to hunt the glowing and terrible Hound of the Baskervilles.

Doyle's genius, which brought Holmes to life, was probably also excited because Doyle was a romantic Victorian gentleman who created in Holmes the embodiment of his chivalric ideals. His son has written that he learned at Doyle's knee "that there are in life three tests of a gentleman: firstly, his attitude of protection and chivalry to women; secondly, his courteous behavior to people of lower social status than himself; and, thirdly, his rectitude in financial matters."

Holmes rarely accepted pay for his work, though he did permit reimbursement of expenses. He was a savior of maidens in distress, and of such men as Hilton Cubitt ("The Adventure of the Dancing Men") who was "a fine creature, this man of the old English soil—simple, straight, and gentle, with his great, earnest blue eyes and broad, comely face. His love for his wife and his trust in her shone in his features." Here Watson serves Doyle by celebrating Doyle himself and the virtues he held dear. The patronizing, amusing side of such virtues is clear in a story such as "The Adventure of the Blue Carbuncle," where Doyle has Holmes conclude from a man's hat, long unbrushed, that his wife has ceased to love him—why else would she fail to brush his hat? And "fallen" women in Doyle's stories always die, whether they have jumped, or have been seduced, from the pinnacle that Doyle's readers saw as respectability.

Doyle presumed that he had made a knight to serve his English ideals, and a man "whose character admits of no light or shade," he said, criticizing Holmes in his autobiography. "He is a calculating machine," Doyle summarized, "and anything you add to that simply weakens the effect." To some extent, Doyle was right. Holmes was machinelike, in the age made great by Romantic ideals coupled with the advance of machinery. Holmes was the protector of order in a world increasingly threatened—by radical movements among the working classes, by a pesky intellectual radicalism among the educated, by exciting ideas about sexual emancipation, and by the rapid growth of increasingly unruly cities in a nation made smaller by railroads—and

Holmes served, while police were thought to fail because they were as inefficient as a government seeming to grow less and less efficient. Holmes did more than serve: he succeeded in protecting the old codes of behavior, the comfortable rules by which the nation had grown. He was the knight of the ancient ways.

But his typically Victorian worship of science, his often cold demeanor that hid the profound activity of his great brain, made him a most extraordinary protector of the ordinary. He was something of a Superman. He was the distant and powerful father, the essence of wisdom and strength. He could descend into a den of murderers and emerge unscathed. He could take six inches off his height through muscular control, could wrinkle his face at will so as to age twenty years, box a bully to unconsciousness, wield a sword like D'Artagnan, see danger where all appeared pacific, outwit the most brilliant of enemies, and read, as Holmes once wrote in an article on deduction, from a tiny drop of water "the possibility of an Atlantic or a Niagara without having seen or heard of one or the other." Contemporary comic characters like Superman, or film heroes such as Indiana Jones, are similarly embodiments of how contemporary readers or viewers see themselves and their society's order, and how they wish to be saved—or have a savior who rescues others on their behalf—with titanic imperviousness. Holmes was such a hero. He is idiosyncratic, interesting, often amusing, and indestructible. He is the chevalier of the railroad carriages and dark streets, of the sour fogs and bloodied bedroom walls.

Though unswerved by sex, Holmes did love once, I would suggest. The first of his great tales, "A Scandal in Bohemia," begins, "To Sherlock Holmes, she is always *the* woman." It is a story of failure. Although Holmes outwits Irene Adler, his foe, the temptress said to threaten European political stability through her dalliance with the king of Bohemia, it is also a story in which Holmes's solution to the problem is not wholly effective—the results desired by the king are achieved, but not the clean victory sought by Holmes. He is outwitted by *the* woman, and she dupes him while she is disguised as a man. He keeps her portrait, a sentimentality that seems different from his collecting trophies of other cases. While in some of those other cases Holmes may fail, he does not fail because of female competition. He is like his Victorian fans: he wishes to champion women, not to endure competition from them. And while he can demonstrate his wit as superior to Watson's, and that of the police, and ours—"You see, but you do not observe," he says; "the distinction is clear"—he cannot see further than Irene Adler. She conquers him sexually, she out- or unmans him, because she beats him *at his trade.*

There shall be no sex, then, for Holmes. There is only the pursuit of malefactors, the service of social order, and the exercise of his enormous wit. At the end of *The Sign of Four,* Watson says, "You have done all the work in this business. I get a wife out of it, Jones [a policeman] gets the credit, pray what remains for you?" And Holmes replies that for him, "There still remains the cocaine-bottle."

That bottle for which Holmes reaches his long white hand is necessary because Holmes is needful of crime and its stimulations. It is the greatest appetite to which he confesses, often skipping meals until he keels over because he doesn't want physical energy diverted from the reasoning process to the process of digestion. Obviously, a hunger for fame—he lets the police take most of the credit—and a hunger for love—he is in all ways too selfless—are not factors in the motivation of Sherlock Holmes. Doyle was the great ordinary Englishman. And therefore Holmes's energy was directed by Doyle away from the distractions, embarrassments and frights—not to mention mere pleasure—of sexuality, and toward another great Victorian hunger: *work.* Sherlock Holmes was made, and by one woman unmade, in terms of work. The late Victorians felt the pressure of the impending twentieth century as a frightening weight. Conan Doyle's reaction—he was to write *The White Company,* a novel of the Middle Ages—was to make his hero Holmes a chaste knight who renounced all appetites but work—and the cocaine that was its only substitute.

What hungers drive Watson? In *Four,* love is a factor. Adventure, to be sure, flogs him on, as do ideas of service and duty. But what of the hungers of the writer, which Watson may derive from his creator? It is Watson who gives us Holmes (not Doyle directly); it is Watson, as well as Holmes, who is noticed in the press for his stories of Holmes's adventures. And it is Watson, a mediocre doctor, an unspectacular man, who rises to heights—on paper—as Holmes does.

We listen, then, as Watson's own literary character, Holmes, complains of how Watson glorifies him. In "The Crooked Man," Holmes has just performed his usual start-of-the-story magic by showing off his knowledge of details about Watson that Watson thought to be un-knowable. He cries out in admiration. Holmes coldly replies that his knowledge is "elementary," and then he says this:

> It is one of those instances where the reasoner can produce an effect which seems remarkable to his neighbour, because the latter has missed the one little point which is the basis of the deduction. The same may be said, my dear fellow, for the effect of some of these little sketches of yours, which is entirely meretricious, *depending as it does upon your retaining in your own hands some factors in the problem which are never imparted to the reader* (my italics).

This is a complaint made over and over, in story after story, by Holmes, and the complaints say that Holmes is not who we think him to be. He may be less "super," less magical, less—as Watson says in "The Greek Interpreter"—"an isolated phenomenon, a brain without a heart"; he is, clearly, more mysterious, a man we cannot know.

For Holmes is complaining to Watson that Watson doesn't report events in their right order, facts in their full light. He withholds what Holmes knows, when Holmes knows it, so that Holmes will seem larger than life *to Watson's readers.* In his private capacity, Watson knows what he knows. In his public function, as writer, Holmes seems to say, Watson withholds what he knows and alters how it becomes known, in order to manipulate those to whom he reports.

The fictional stories of Holmes and Watson are, within their frame-works, also stories about how reality is discerned, examined and dis-cussed. On a small scale, Doyle gives us fiction-about-fiction. Students of Barth or Borges might be tempted to call them metafictions. We can do no less than resist such temptations on behalf of readers everywhere, while reserving to ourselves a small expression of pleasure at the complexities in the work of an often underrated Conan Doyle.

There is also this complexity to be honored: Doyle wished to write historical novels and accounts of his travels and, most important to him, accounts of his spiritualist researches; he tired early of Holmes, and I believe that he saw himself as trading his talents for a mess of pottage. It seems certain to me that Doyle, who saw aspects of himself in both Watson and Holmes, chastised himself in print when he made Holmes chastise the doctor and writer John Watson. *You are writing meretricious stuff,* Doyle scolds himself. *You use cheap tricks, you don't write what you should.* History was a wiser judge than the writer himself, as so often is the case. History tolerates the spiritualism; it celebrates those "little sketches of yours."

Before his fictive death, Holmes describes Dr. Moriarty, whom Holmes is about to undo: "This man's occupation's gone," he says, in "The Final Problem." He is paraphrasing Othello. And after his return from the grave, in the story called "The Adventure of the Norwood Builder," Holmes describes himself as "the poor out-of-work specialist, whose occupation has gone." These statements are remarkable enough from the man who Watson once thought knew "nil" about literature. More remarkable is that Othello cries, "Farewell! Othello's occupation's gone!" because he is unmanned as a warrior, having begun to believe that his wife is unfaithful to him; his work—as fighter, as general—is predicated, now, upon the orderliness of the love between Othello and Desdemona. So we have Holmes describing the absence of the stimulation that his vocation offers in terms used by an outraged husband and warrior who bids farewell to sexual love and the profession of war.

For Holmes, the game that is afoot *is* his "occupation"; it is the repository of his sexual, domestic and most bellicose energies. His feelings toward crime are as Othello's toward marriage and trust. In his need for his work, Holmes is as huge as the raging soldier. And somehow that single-mindedness, the carrying within him of society's anger at disorder, its need for a hero, its wish for older virtues—all these traditional values are sustained by Holmes, and by us as well.

Holmes lives. He is written about, both in parodies and in celebrations; he exists in fiction and in learned tracts; letters addressed to Holmes at 221B Baker Street continue to arrive at the London Post Office; he is shown in old films and new, and he is presented in television productions. He cannot die. Even his creator could not kill him. There is the gasogene, there is the Turkish slipper filled with strong tobacco, there is the hypodermic needle, there the heavy stick. He begins for us in 1887, an eccentric experimenter in a laboratory, meeting a frail John Watson, lately attached to the Berkshires in Afghanistan, where he was wounded; and he remains with us through the 1927 *Casebook of Sherlock Holmes,* a semiretired keeper of bees. In one of his later stories, "His Last Bow," Holmes says, "Good old Watson! You are the one fixed point in a changing age."

But Holmes's last bow is not, of course, his last. A final volume follows. And even the final story of *that* volume, "The Adventure of the

Retired Colourman," is not his last. For Holmes, also a fixed point in
our changing age, somehow continues. He goes on in part because
of Doyle's craft, and in part because readers need a Holmes, someone whose occupation is, as we're told in "The Speckled Band,"
"to see deeply into the manifold wickedness of the human heart."
Such wickedness is in part *our* hidden occupation. Holmes knows it.

But might Conan Doyle regret such a statement? Might he not wish
to have reported, to himself and to his readers, that courage and de-
cency and chaste self-sacrifice obtained, and not what Holmes, perhaps against his creator's wishes, ferreted out? Thus Doyle might, using
Holmes's fictive voice and reasons, have scolded Watson, the writer side
of Conan Doyle. Thus Sir Arthur Conan Doyle, wishing to work as a
doctor—or, anyway, knowing his failure as one—and wishing to write
of gentle virtues and gentlemen, wishing to report on voices from the
other side of death (not the voices of those who ministered it), might
have lamented himself, and the disappearance of *his* occupation. Like
Viktor Frankenstein's creature circling the globe in pursuit of his creator, Holmes pursued Conan Doyle across the pages of his books.
Doyle tried to murder his character Holmes, but Holmes relentlessly
followed, in spite of the writer's godlike powers to shut life down.
Holmes reads the hearts of his readers today. He read his creator's
from the start. The writer's horror over such rebellion, I'd suggest,
lingers. So that we *know* Holmes knows our darknesses.

·§ THE WHALE AS §· SHAGGY DOG

In *Advertisements for Myself* Norman Mailer tells how he came to write "The Man Who Studied Yoga." He had been experiencing difficulty, in 1951 and 1952, in placing his short fiction in magazines, and when a story ("The Paper House") was being considered by one of the large women's magazines, friends brought that magazine's editor to a party at Mailer's apartment. When the party was done, Mailer says, he realized that the editor had been "condescending." He had a sense of having sunk to pandering to magazine editors. Furthermore, he felt the futility of trying to place his writing in "the slicks": "One would have to win the Nobel Prize before a fashion magazine would like a heroine who was a whorehouse whore."

The evening was cathartic. Disgusted with the literary marketplace, with a sense of himself as an "amateur literary politician," Mailer woke the next morning with a literary scheme worthy, he felt, of a real artist. Instead of "trying to write less than I knew," he says, he awakened to a feeling that he must be "getting ready for something too large." The "something" was

> a prologue and an eight-part novel . . . the prologue to be the day of a small frustrated man, a minor artist manqué. The eight novels were to be eight stages of his dream later that night, and the books would revolve around the adventures of a mythical hero, Sergius O'Shaugnessy, who would travel through many worlds, through pleasure, business, communism, church, working class, crime, homosexuality and mysticism.

Only part of this giant dream was fulfilled. As Mailer writes in his Advertisement (written during 1958 and 1959 for *Advertisements for*

Myself), he decided to forget the eight-novel scheme while he was finishing the first draft of *The Deer Park:* he felt "I had a novel to work on, and a good prologue which could stand as a short novel, and so it was not too difficult to admit I was not ready."

He stands by his prologue-become-short-novel, calling it one of several "thirty-page fragments . . . from that long novel which has come into my mind again, a descendant of Moby Dick which will call for such time, strength, cash and patience that I do not know if I have it all to give. . . ."

The prologue, often reprinted in anthologies now as a long short story, is often re-read, and it usually confounds. And it is difficult for readers to see the sad tale of Sam Slovoda as "a descendant of Moby Dick." But I would like to suggest that it is and that the narrative method, as well as a crucial small event in the story, descends directly from the narrator Ishmael in *Moby-Dick,* and from small Pippin, the black cabin boy who jumps from a whaling boat and drifts alone for hours in the sea—of whom Melville's Ishmael says, "The sea had jeeringly kept his finite body up, but drowned the infinite of his soul."

The narrative voice of "The Man Who Studied Yoga" introduces himself in this way: "I would introduce myself if it were not useless. The name I had last night will not be the same as the name I have tonight." The voice then goes on to tell the story of Sam Slovoda, failure:

> He has tried too many things and never with a whole heart. He has wanted to be a serious novelist and now merely indulges the ambition; he wished to be of consequence in the world, and has ended, temporarily perhaps, as an overworked writer of continuity for comic magazines; when he was young he tried to be a bohemian and instead acquired a wife and family.

Sam's situation is not so different from Mailer's at the start of writing his Prologue: he himself feels failed, inconsequential; he caters (or so he fears) to the ludicrous ladies' magazines. Furthermore, the narrative voice of "The Man" goes on, "He is in the process of being psychoanalyzed. Myself, I do not jeer. It has created the most unusual situation between Sam and me." It seems entirely possible that Mailer the writer is also psychoanalyzing himself, or at least studying himself, as he creates a voice which might speak for him about Sam, who might in some ways represent him.

The problem for Mailer, then, seems clear as he begins his work. He must write about a character whose problems are apparently parallel (in some ways) to his. Like all writers, to some degree, he must write about himself. And yet, in the interests of creating a fiction (not autobiography), he must objectify his own voice. In the interests of satisfying the writer's need for self-analysis while not confusing himself with his character, he must be both in and out of the story simultaneously. The narrative voice he has constructed is the solution to his problem—a first-person voice that is, nevertheless, omniscient in ability to see (through boundaries of time and place, into dreams and thoughts). Thus the "I" of the story reads Sam's thoughts, recalls his memories, watches Sam and his wife Eleanor in their intimacies. He offers their feelings—*and his own.* He analyzes them and, as he does so, analyzes himself.

At the beginning of the story's action, the narrative voice says that to introduce himself is "useless." At the end of the story, he reveals himself as a character in it by realizing that he can (or, even, that he must) introduce himself. As Sam falls asleep, the narrator—hovering like a god or ghost—watches him, reads his thoughts. Sam recalls his unfinished novel and sees that it is "a formless wreck of incidental ideas and half-episodes, utterly without shape." One wonders if, at the time of writing, Mailer's own eight-novel scheme might not have seemed to be in similar shape. Then Sam goes on to lament that he has not even a hero for his book:

> One could not have a hero today, Sam thinks, a man of action and contemplation, capable of sin, large enough for good, a man immense. . . . One needs a man who could walk the stage, someone who—no matter who, not himself. Someone, Sam thinks, who reasonably could not exist.

It is after this moment that the narrator says, "I give an idea to Sam. 'Destroy time, and chaos may be ordered,' I say to him." Apparently the narrator now feels that it is not "useless" to "introduce" himself— and he does, directly into the fabric of the story. It is as if the voice has understood his own usefulness; it is as if he has seen that he might "walk the stage" for Sam—or that Sam might walk it for him—and so he moves from his apparent aloofness to action in his own tale: he creates himself before our eyes, just as he does Sam.

For Sam's lamentation over his lack of hero is precisely a description

of the narrator himself: someone both good and bad, active and con-
templative, "immense," someone who can "walk the stage," someone
who is not Sam himself—someone who "reasonably could not exist."
With this last description, it seems, Sam has not only described the
narrator, given birth to him as an artist gives birth to his character
(and as the character, his narrator, may have given birth to *him*); he has
led us (and, perhaps, Mailer) to see the sort of hero Mailer's eight-
novel opus will require: someone who can be present and yet not be
present, a new voice for saying fiction, a new way of being intimately
involved as writer while being objectively aloof—like a third-person
omniscient voice. The narrator is Sam's other self, waiting to be born.
He is born, at the end of the story, but he is born to a "writer man-
qué": Sam, instead of leaping up to write his creation, falls asleep, and
the creation is stillborn. He leaves the narrator to say, "What a dreary
compromise is life!" and disappear, as did the alter ego narrator of
Melville's "Bartleby," crying "Ah Bartleby! Ah humanity!"—as perhaps does Mailer, realizing potential failure even as he (like Sam)
makes his artistic discovery. "I do not know," Mailer writes of his
eight-book project, "if I have it all to give, and so will skip the separate
parts, avoid the dream, and try a more modest ascent on the spiral of
Time."

Certainly, Melville's *Moby-Dick* is also a story of a man trying to give
birth to himself, whereas the narrative voice of that effort is partly
his, and partly his author's. Mailer would hasten to add, surely, that
Melville's story is far greater than his. But he might be willing to
agree—indeed his reference to Moby Dick in the Advertisement pro-
vokes the comparison—that there are parallel elements in "The Man
Who Studied Yoga" and the greatest American work of fiction.

Whereas Mailer's narrator begins by obliterating his own importance (or seeming to), with his strange, "I would introduce myself
if it were not useless," Melville's, of course, begins with the self-
proclaiming "Call me Ishmael." The one begins as "nothing" and
nearly becomes a whole; the other, I would like to suggest, begins
deceptively as a whole person, undergoes fragmentation, and is reborn—as a new whole, in danger of fragmentation once more. The
Mailer narrator ends as still-divided. The Melville narrator ends the
same way.

"Call me Ishmael" is deceptive. We are to "call" him his evocative name as if he were an entire and unified person. But he clearly is not. At a troubled time of his own life, Melville creates a character whose "splintered heart and maddened hand were turned against the wolfish world." This sense of self and of the cosmos is the novel's pivoting point; it is repeated throughout. The splintered man who thinks that he finds peace (unity) in a manly marriage to savage Queequeg—"we were married"; "our hearts' honeymoon"; their "household joy"— finds over and over that he still is a man divided. Melville, too, is a man divided as he sets about writing his book. He must please his readers and earn enough to support his family, and yet he must satisfy his need to deal with the blackness of darkness beyond. He sums up the problem in writing to Richard Dana, author of *Two Years Before the Mast*, ". . . did I not write these books of mine almost entirely for 'lucre'—by the job, as a woodsawyer saws wood," and then says this:

> It will be a strange sort of book, tho', I fear; blubber is blubber you
> know; tho' you may get oil out of it, the poetry runs as hard as sap
> from a frozen maple tree;— & to cook the thing up, one must
> needs throw in a little fancy, which from the nature of the thing,
> must be ungainly as the gambols of the whales themselves. Yet
> I mean to give the truth of the thing, in spite of this.

His division of interests is similar to his division of artistic needs. Like Mailer, a hundred years later, he seeks a way of speaking of his own confused self and of his fictive world—of bridging them, yet keeping them separate. In the Shakespeare he is discovering, Melville finds the key to sustaining that creative tension:

> But it is those deep far-away things in him; those occasional
> flashings-forth of the intuitive Truth in him; those short quick
> probings at the very axis of reality:—these are the things that
> make Shakespeare, Shakespeare. Through the mouths of the dark
> characters of Hamlet, Timon, Lear, and Iago, he craftily says, or
> sometimes insinuates the things, which we feel to be so terrifically
> true, that it were all but madness for any good man, in his own
> proper character, to utter, or even hint of them.

How similar this is to Sam Slovoda's need for "a man immense. . . . One needs a man who could walk the stage, someone who—no matter who, not himself." And Melville makes a character, as did Mailer, who is not himself and who yet embodies his dilemmas, who walks the stage, is immense, larger than the traditional limitations of point-of-view. For as Mailer's narrator is fragmented, and a voice with the properties of both first- and third-person, so is Mailer's model: Melville and his splintered Ishmael.

While he fluctuates between feelings of peace (soon after his "marriage" to Queequeg) and cosmic dread as, one hundred pages later, he feels "the problem of the universe revolving in me," Ishmael is more than *this* set of problems. He overhears Ahab speak while Ahab is on deck and Ishmael is not. He hears Stubb speak to Flask while they are ostensibly alone. Starbuck soliloquizes and Ishmael somehow hears. He transcends the limitations of his first-person situation, and so often, when he does so, the characters on whom he reports "walk the stage": there is chapter 29, titled "Enter Ahab; to him, Stubb"; there is chapter 36, subtitled "*(Enter Ahab: Then, all.)*". In that chapter there is Ahab speaking in what the narrator, Ishmael, labels as "*(Aside)*"; in chapter 37 we have the dramatic subtitle, "*(The cabin; by the stern windows; Ahab sitting alone, and gazing out.).*" Just as Slovoda is the narrator's other side, and the narrator in part his creation, and just as both enact the drama of Mailer the writer, so is Ahab the dramatic creation of Ishmael—or the dramatic reinterpretation Ishmael makes of his captain. (Whereas Melville in the letter to Dana uses this construction: ". . . the things that make Shakespeare, Shakespeare," Ishmael has his captain use this one: "Is Ahab, Ahab? Is it I, God, or who, that lifts this arm." Where Ahab questions the motivating force behind him, Melville, with parallel construction, is speaking of a probing "at the very axis of reality" by an author whose characters speak on behalf of his darkest self.) Ishmael forces the men on his doomed ship to "walk the stage" in enactment of his darker side. They say, or insinuate, "the things, which we feel to be so terrifically true, that it were all but madness for any good man, *in his own proper character*, to utter, or even hint . . ." (my italics). The pun on "proper character" holds up, I think. Ishmael, Melville's character, so representative of his own doubts and needs, creates, or imposes his imagination upon, these "dark characters"—Ahab, Starbuck, Queequeg, Fedallah—and renders them the dramatic participants in his own tragedy. When Ahab, whose hubris terrifies Ishmael (and yet in whose black communion pledge Ishmael drinks), is dead, then Ishmael is reborn—free, he and we might think, of his darker doubting side.

And yet this is not wholly so. Mailer's short story is the tale of a writer who fails. The narrator is a side of that writer, partly his shaping spirit, who organizes the telling of the story of the story-teller. It is art about art. And the same is true of Melville's monumental tale. Although Ahab, "a man immense . . . who could walk the stage, someone . . . not himself," is apparently vanished, Ishmael the narrator is left to tell us his story. And it frightens him, even in the telling. Like Slovoda, who dives into sleep to escape his narrator-induced insights, Ishmael, throughout his story, dives into cetology and the "realistic" data of sailing on a whaler so as to evade the insights—his compulsion to dwell on them—which he himself, as narrator, sees, while he tells his tale.

His is the Elizabethan malady: melancholic speculation. And it visits him while he is least prepared. In the central portion of his story, the middle chapters in which we learn how whales are killed and stored, Ishmael buries himself—as teller of his adventure. He tries to evade what he knows he knows. And so, while speaking of the whale's skin, "The Blanket," as he calls it, the outer layer of that symbol for the veil his Ahab-self saw imprisoning man, he says, "It is transparent, as I said before; and being laid upon the printed page, I have sometimes pleased myself with fancying it exerted a magnifying influence." He tries to move away from a looming insight with the next sentence: "At any rate, it is pleasant to read about whales through their own spectacles, as you may say." But he cannot escape, and shortly he says of the marks found on the skins of killed whales, "Like those mystic rocks [palisades on the upper Mississippi], too, the mystic-marked whale remains undecipherable."

He is trying not to see what he saw, trying not to scrutinize as, on his soul's voyage, he did scrutinize. He is afraid to lay the experience, like transparent whale's skin, "upon the printed page." He wishes not to say fully (or write) what he *really* saw, or tried to see. He wishes, at this point of the story, to avoid the sense he has for a while shrugged off—that there is no escape from his questing Ahab-self. Speaking as a writer in his own tale, Ishmael has already tried to excuse his apparent excessive use of realistic material:

So ignorant are most landsmen of some of the plainest and most palpable wonders of the world, that without some hints touching the plain facts, historical and otherwise, of the fishery, they might scout at Moby Dick as a monstrous fable, or still worse and more detestable, a hideous and intolerable allegory.

Ishmael the narrator says that he wishes the whale named Moby Dick to be seen in a realistic context; hence he buries his reader, and his own doubts, in the sometimes distracting "plain facts." But the book is also named Moby Dick, and it is Ishmael, after his journey, as he dwells on the horrors he perceived, who wishes to protect himself. *He* does not want to see what he learned of himself or the world. *He* does not want "a monstrous fable" or "intolerable allegory"; and "monstrous" and "intolerable" do not apply to a reader's pejorative judgments: they accurately reflect Ishmael's own fear of what he knows. So he hides. And so does Sam Slovoda—who is the other side of his perceptive narrator.

In the parent work, *Moby-Dick*, and in its literary descendant, "The Man Who Studied Yoga," we may then see similar concerns: the troubled author who feels somewhat divided; a resultant work in which the characters reflect that division; a narrator who both includes and excludes the personal problems of the writer; a narrator who is part artist and who renders dramatic his own fragmentation by creating his other self before the reader's eyes. There are other descendants of that parent work in the Mailer canon. But before referring to them, it is useful to look at the most direct and obvious debt Mailer owes to Melville: the mad revelations in "The Man Who Studied Yoga."

Pippin, called Pip, jumps overboard in *Moby-Dick*. Panicked during the fury of a whale chase, he leaps from his boat and is left behind. For long hours he drifts on an empty sea, abandoned, to be rescued only by chance. (These events are parallel to those of Ishmael's escape from the *Pequod*'s fate.) Speaking of the dreadful solitude of such an experience, Ishmael says, "The intense concentration of self in the middle of such a heartless immensity, my God! who can tell it?" Pip returns, an apparent idiot. In truth, he has seen the wonders of the world, and he returns as a kind of maddened Fool, who speaks the Truth: "He saw God's foot upon the treadle of the loom, and spoke it; and therefore his shipmates called him mad. So man's insanity is heaven's sense." One must wonder if the analogy between Pip's and Ishmael's "fall" and "rebirth" suggests that Ishmael has become maddened, like Pip; if so, the novel, his story, may be taken as a "sane madness," which is what Melville ascribes to Lear in his essay on Hawthorne.

Later, Pip speaks his "sense." And the first time is before the gold doubloon Ahab has nailed to his mast, promising it to the first sailor who spies Moby Dick. Ishmael in this ninety-ninth chapter dramatizes the reactions of Ahab and the mates, Queequeg and others, to the doubloon. It obviously becomes the emblem of each man's sense of the universe: Ahab sees it only in terms of representations of Ahab; Starbuck sees in it holy signs; a morbid Manxman sees in it doom. Pip, in his first public utterance since his catastrophe, describes the doubloon precisely in terms of Ishmael's dilemma; once again Ishmael makes a darker character walk the stage and speak for him:

> Here's the ship's navel, this doubloon here, and they are all on fire to unscrew it. But, unscrew your navel, and what's the consequence? Then again, if it stays here, that is ugly, too, for when aught's nailed to the mast it's a sign that things grow desperate.

This is Ishmael's axis of decision: to unscrew the doubloon, see the possible horror on the other side of the veil (since the man who unscrews the doubloon has found Moby Dick and precipitated the voyage into dread); or to leave it on the mast and grow "desperate" with his willed ignorance of the horror. It is the decision to be made by Ishmael the story-teller as he assembles his narrative. Shall he expose himself to what he saw or imagined? Shall he dive deeper into his "monstrous fable"? He makes his fateful decision and in chapter 100, directly after Pip's speech, a passing ship, the *Enderby*, points the *Pequod* toward Moby Dick and disaster.

In "The Man Who Studied Yoga," friends have come to Slovoda's home to show a pornographic film. (It will later stimulate him and Eleanor to make love in grotesque imitation of the pornographic parody of lovemaking: false artist imitating false art in a story about artistic failure.) Its scenes of make-believe sexual victimization (in which the victim's name is also Eleanor) correspond directly with Sam's recollection—as he falls asleep, away from art and its dangers—of a friend of Eleanor who is in a mental institution. Mad, like Pip, she babbles that "every night when the doors are locked, they come to my room and they make the movie. I am the heroine and am subjected to all variety of sexual viciousness. Tell them to leave me alone so I may enter the convent." The mad voice, it seems to me, corresponds directly with Pip's mad revelation of his narrator's dilemma. For this mad voice recounts what has happened in the film; in a sense, then, it is "true." If we accept the correspondence between Pip and Eleanor's friend, we see that, while Ishmael sees the truth-in-madness and cannot evade it, Sam succeeds in evading his truth: he hides in sleep. The truth, here, concerns evasion of reality, taking refuge in pretense—thus this description of the film-watchers: "The audience sways, each now finally lost in himself, communing hungrily with shadows, violated or violating, fantasy triumphant." One might say the same of Ahab and his mates as they study the doubloon.

Ishmael cannot hide for long. But Slovoda does hide in his own shadows; he fantasizes, and cannot dare life. Thus his lovemaking is parodistic of parody; he and Eleanor pretend: they do not meet each other. And so Sam's art has declined from the risks of making a hero, destroying time's limitations, ordering chaos—into writing for comic strips. He *is* a comic strip, the outlines of a man and artist; his substance, his narrator, floats above him, a ghost condemned to wander.

But before the film is shown, and before even these potential matrices for insight are exposed to Sam, the couples in his living room embarrassedly chatter, as if to prove that they need not see the film right away, as if their voyeuristic lust were not strong. The talk turns to Mailer's proposed hero who will walk the stage for him and be "not himself" while still expressing him—Sergius O'Shaugnessy, here called Cassius O'Shaugnessy. One character, Alan, tells how their friend O'Shaugnessy, "a psychopath," as mad as Pip seemed to *his* friends, reappears after a long absence. He has traveled to India to study yoga and has returned with this story:

> "I was sitting on my haunches contemplating my navel . . . when of a sudden I discovered my navel under a different aspect. It seemed to me that if I were to give a counter-clockwise twist, my navel would unscrew. . . . Taking a deep breath, I turned, and the abysses of Vishtarni loomed beneath. My navel had begun to unscrew. I knew I was about to accept the reward of three years of contemplation. So . . . I turned and I turned . . . and after a period I knew that with one more turn my navel would unscrew itself forever. At the edge of revelation, I took one sweet breath, and turned my navel free."
>
> Alan looks up at his audience.
>
> "Damn," said Cassius, "if my ass didn't fall off."

Here then is the revelation of *Moby-Dick:* its wisdom becomes a vulgar
joke in "The Man Who Studied Yoga." The whale becomes a shaggy
dog. Prophecy becomes nonsense. And, more important, the nonsense
is also prophetic: it warns Sam not to dare to unscrew the doubloon,
not to annihilate time—note that Cassius unscrews his navel counter-
clockwise, in reversal of time—and not to look at the horror that
might, as insight, present itself. As the doubloon is the ship's navel in
Moby-Dick—tragedy is nourished through it—so it is in Mailer's story.
For Pip also describes the navel as human: "unscrew *your* navel" (my
italics). Just as it is emblematic of each crew member's interpretation
of the world, the point through which their world view receives sustenance, so it is for Sam Slovoda an emblem of his world view. He learns
from the psychopath's story that his world view is "correct." The
wisdom of three years' study—Ishmael shipped out on a three-year
voyage—is that courage and energy spent in annihilating time are to
no avail: one can end up further severed from himself than when he
began. The tragedy here (which Slovoda's other self does see) is that
without risk and energy there is only fantasy, an illusion of wholeness,
an eternal slumber. So Sam and the narrator remain cleft: Sam pro-
nounces that "modern life is schizoid." Sam compromises, as Ishmael
finally could not. The one falls into a kind of death—"I do not feel my
nose, my nose is numb, my eyes are heavy, my eyes are heavy"—while
the other voyages on to face his fears.

Mailer also voyaged on. In *The Deer Park*, concentration on which
drove Mailer away from his eight-volume scheme, the protagonist is
the Sergius O'Shaugnessy on whom Mailer had counted as his hero.
Sergius is a first-person narrator who, nevertheless, relates the most
intimate histories and reasonings of the people he meets in Southern
California. For the major portion of the novel, Mailer's hero of bin-
ocular vision accounts for his (physically) impossible insights by claiming to have spent long hours in listening to his new acquaintances relate their pasts: "He would tell story after story"; ". . . he was forced
to be a lonely man, and a good part of our friendship was due to the
fact that I looked for his company"; "In an hour he told me one story
after another, acting all the parts and creating person after person by
no more than a move of his hands." Mailer writes *The Deer Park* as if
he wants to create a narrator like that of "The Man Who Studied
Yoga," and yet does not dare to. So his first-person narrator, who does

know as much as a third-person voice, makes these excuses for his knowledge. The narrator (who wishes to become a writer), like Mailer, slides away from the fact that he is inventing darker characters to walk the stage for him. Both Mailer and his protagonist behave like Sam Slovoda. In his Advertisement for excerpts of the novel in *Advertisements for Myself* Mailer tells how

> originally *The Deer Park* had been about a movie director and a girl with whom he had a bad affair, and it was told by a sensitive but faceless young man. In changing the young man, I saved the book from being minor, but put a disproportion upon it because my narrator became too interesting, and not enough happened to him in the second half of the book.

Actually, what happened was that the spirit of the narrator of "The Man Who Studied Yoga" took eminence, and "not enough" happened to the narrator of *The Deer Park* in its second half because its narrator, acting on Mailer's behalf, began to invent darker characters and events to speak for him. Marion Faye, the novel's bisexual psychopath, plays a more prominent role in the second half—as Sergius invents his thoughts (the way Ishmael rendered Ahab) and has Marion, a Tiresias, speak on his behalf. Sergius (and Mailer) no longer make excuses for his knowledge of the intimate affairs of others. As Mailer rewrote the book at a very rapid pace to meet his publisher's deadline, his Sergius became similar to Melville's Ishmael, and to his descendant, the narrator of "The Man Who Studied Yoga."

At the end of *The Deer Park*, Sergius—on the other side of America, now, while his friend Eitel is still in California—shows us Eitel ("I-tell") driving home from work, then stepping onto his balcony to look at the sea:

> He had come along that road tonight on the drive back to his house, and he remembered how at a stoplight, just before the neon signs and the hamburger stands and the tourist camps which threw up their shoddy skirts to the capital, he had stared out across the water and seen a freighter with its holdlights and its mast-lamps moving away to the horizon. It was off on a voyage and the men who sailed it would look for adventure.
>
> Almost idly, for the first time in many months, Eitel thought of me then, and wondered, "Is Sergius possibly on that boat?"

Then the light changed to green and he raced his motor and rode away and forgot the freighter.

Eitel thinks back once more to the freighter, then thinks with a pang of "the end of his overextended youth."

What happens here is that Mailer and Sergius once more learn the lesson of that shaping spirit in "The Man Who Studied Yoga." Sergius is here creating the experience of Eitel before our eyes; he invents Charlie Eitel and his thoughts: Charlie is his character, and so is Sergius, here, his own character as well. The one middle-aged, the other young; the one conceived of as shipping out (like Ishmael) to adventure, the other conceiving of himself as standing still; the one learning the limitations of his life, the other defeated by them—these opposing traits are really oxymoronic, coexisting as they do in the same narrator-character (and, very possibly, in their author as well).

Furthermore, Sergius has learned the lesson Sam Slovoda hears as he falls to sleep: "Destroy time, and chaos may be ordered." For a metaphor for time, Mailer uses the green traffic light. In Eitel's imagination (his re-creation of the event *after* the fact: an artistic annihilation of time in itself), Sergius had gone on while, at the traffic light, he, Eitel, stood still. But the event is created in the first place by Sergius, who reports to us after it has purportedly occurred; part of himself races into his past while the other speeds forward—all in an artwork (his narrative) that assaults time, since it creates the events for us in a time-destroying illusion. The traffic light is Fitzgerald's "green light, the orgiastic future that year by year recedes before us."

And still Mailer voyaged on, this time in 1967, with *Why Are We in Vietnam?*, ostensibly the story of an Alaskan bear hunt. Here, the hunted bear is doubloon; the narrator, D.J.,

> was in love with himself because he did not wish to scream or plead, he just wished to encounter Mr. D., big-ass grizz, and the next step put his nose into an aisle of forest scents, herbs offering each their high priest of here, here is the secret lore and the cold fires of the temple . . . the tenderness of the tip where life began. . . .
> That was when the grizz came.

The quest is for self and the American language. Across a frontier (psychic and geographical) go the narrator, D.J., and his intimate friend, Tex Hyde; they are—Jekyll and Hyde—each other's alter ego.

D.J. tells us of their quest, and then reminds us (directly and through the book's concern for radio transmission, and its division into sequences of a radio broadcast) that D.J. is also the acronym for disc jockey. He reminds us that he is broadcasting himself to us—is very possibly, as the narrator, also creating himself as we listen:

> I will merely offer this clue—we have no material physical site
> or locus for this record, because I can be in the act of writing it,
> recording it, slipping it (all unwitting to myself) into the tran-
> sistorized aisles and microfilm of the electronic Lord (who, if he
> is located in the asshole, must be Satan) or I can be expiring con-
> sciousness, I can be the unwindings and unravelings of a nervous
> constellation just now executed, killed, severed or stopped, maybe
> even stunned, who thunders, Herman Melville go hump Moby and
> wash his Dick.
>
> Or maybe I'm a Spade and writing like a Shade. . . . Some ge-
> nius brain up in Harlem pretending to write a white man's fink
> fuck book in revenge. . . . So you can't know if I'm true-blue
> Wasp-ass Texas even if I know. . . .

The narrative voice itself is split (as is the country of the book, as are its characters); the mode of narration itself enacts the problems of the novel: the narrator creates characters (including himself) as we watch. They "walk the stage" and speak his darker thoughts.

Elements of this concern, by the way, are to be found in *An American Dream* (1965) and in the story "The Time of Her Time" (1958–1959), which is evocative of portions of the concluding parts of *The Deer Park*. In the story, the protagonist is Sergius O'Shaugnessy once more. He has a tempestuous love affair with a girl who accuses him of being homosexual (like Faye, the psychopath). She is revealed to be Sergius's darker side, and—to echo Slovoda's concern about his novel—"a hero fit for me." In *An American Dream* the darker character is physically dark, as D.J. suggests in the passage quoted above from *Why Are We in Vietnam?*. Rojack and Shago, a black psychopath, love the same woman in *An American Dream*. They share (in Shago's black phallic umbrella) similar fetishes and senses of magic. While fighting they embrace, and Rojack finds in Shago's odor "a smell of full near-ness as if we'd been in bed for an hour." The sense of male marriage we find in Ishmael is present here, and one could build a case for

Shago as Rojack's Queequeg. (Mailer might have studied Hawthorne, too. The devilish "fellow-traveler" who escorts Young Goodman Brown to Satan carries a maple stick which speeds Brown to the Black Sabbath at which he learns the worst about his wife and himself. Shago's umbrella permits Rojack to confront the Satanic Kelly high above Manhattan where he learns the dreadful truth about his wife and himself and where the moon looks like a "silvery whale.")

Mailer's next fiction is the prize-winning *The Executioner's Song*, and it is related to *Moby-Dick* and Mailer's fictions written in its wake only by its size and point of view. Mailer listened to hundreds of hours of taped interviews, read hundreds of pages of transcripts, and then entered the minds of murderers and victims as if he were their god. The novel, *or* journalism—there simply is no such beast as a "nonfiction novel"—is fascinating for its insights into killers and into the men and women who stood to make so much money from a killer's life and death; it is instructive too for its hints at Mailer's fascination with murder.

And then, in 1983, comes *Ancient Evenings*, perhaps the very novel Mailer had in mind as he speculated—prayed?—about a huge work of fiction that would be his own "descendant of Moby Dick." The child *is* father to the man. Mailer told us in 1959 that he envisioned a novel made of "eight adventures of a mythical hero . . . who would travel through many worlds." The project seemed to have died, but, three years later, decrying contemporary living, he wrote, "It is a deadened existence, afraid of violence, cannibalism, loneliness, insanity, libidinousness, hell, perversion, and mess, because those are the states which must in some way be passed through, digested, transcended, if one is to make one's way back to life."

In *Ancient Evenings*, what Mailer delivers seems to have been coming over so many years—a very long novel composed of seven (not eight) books, in which the Ka, "one of the seven souls and spirits of the living," according to the novel, which is lumpy with information, confronts the seven essential states of its owner's being, roaring with pain, violence, perversion and mess.

The narrator is Menenhetet, who has just died as the novel begins. Through the good offices and magic of his great-grandfather, who also fathered him, Menenhetet sees much of the story of his own life, of his great-grandfather's life, of ancient Egypt, of the stories of the gods, of the politics of Egyptian kingdoms, and of the soul's progress from death and its rending pain toward a kind of wholeness.

Mailer's prose dances and crackles. Sometimes, though, it does so in the service of what can only be called *longeurs*. Menenhetet One, the great-grandfather, tells stories for the sake of the re-education of Menenhetet Two's Ka (he is our protagonist); so, through the elder's voice, and while Menenhetet Two hears and sees the information the elder gives him, we learn. It is very often like a schoolroom, or a researcher's notebook. We hear and hear and hear, and the mind becomes clotted with data—and with stories about beings we do not know: it is all quite two-dimensional, like glyphs, in fact, on a wall. Always, though, Mailer's energy, his habitual diction (the "gravies" of this, the "marrow" of that, the "sauces" of the other), and his sense that what he says is important, do serve to force the novel along.

Oral love, male and female buggery, the holiness of the orgasm: they are present here, as they were in "The White Negro," *An American Dream* and *Why Are We in Vietnam?*. One accepts that they are part of Mailer's paraphernalia. Always, though, the superb headlong style and even its repetitive, less lovable mannerisms of limb and language were at the service of what Mailer would variously call Time or History or God or the Devil, but which finally would be revealed as the United States of America. Norman Mailer is an artist in love with his nation and its travails, and he took them—along with the Manifest Destiny he shamelessly and beguilingly spelled out in *Of a Fire on the Moon*— for the metaphors of his fiction. His work is intimately tied to the American language and American history. In *The Armies of the Night* he wrote a lover's complaint to the nation, and some of his finest prose.

Here, in Egypt, Mailer is homeless, he is in captivity—enslaved by his abstractions of gods and devils, anuses and excrement, cowardice and courage, and even his own thirty-year-old rhythms and syntactical oppositions: "and so I do not know if I will labor in greed forever among the demonic or serve some noble purpose I cannot name." Small scenes and moments and phrases of this seven-hundred-page novel are, of course, brilliant—there is a lovemaking with Nefertiti that is stunning (she reminds one a bit of Lulu in "The Deer Park")— for Mailer's talent at its worst level of achievement can do more on the page, and has, than an army of quotidian novelists.

But we are not gods, nor are we dead; and we do not share the vocabulary of birth and rebirth, avatars and holy battles, that Mailer has acquired for this novel. We can comprehend the wanderings of the dead, the lovemakings of goddesses, the holinesses of foul old men, only if we are given analogies that draw upon our experience. But Mailer ignores us, and our world, and insists that what matters is only in the high opera world of the mighty, the dead and the fabulous. *Family*, in other words, and *mother, father, lover, mate*—these remain only words on characters' lips. They do not become part of a domestic metaphor that might enable us to *feel* about the giants in this giant novel that works only at the level of abstraction. It is possible that the corruption of the domestic unit was at the heart of *The Executioner's Song* and that Mailer's domestic concerns remain in that book, exhausted for now.

The family, in *Tough Guys Don't Dance*, is dead and gone, though a tough, admired father remains. And though Mailer celebrates his beloved Provincetown—there are fine descriptions of a coastline that Ishmael might have known—there is no Moby Dick, or scent of Melville, or hint of Mailer's own pursuit of his American master. Although Melville has threatened more of what began—or concluded—in *Ancient Evenings*, it does not emerge in a novel said by some cynics to have been written in order to satisfy one contract, or to break another. A number, too large a number, of doggy reviewers have wagged their tails and given *Tough Guys* hyperbolic reviews. Mailer, the president of PEN, the Establishment in New York for writers, is apparently too established to be attacked. For *Tough Guys Don't Dance*, he should be.

Whereas in *The Executioner's Song* Mailer serves several personas, to whom his impulses, metaphors and rhythms must be subservient—

> Outside the blacksmith shop, there was grass and some fruit trees, and the fall-into-heaven of a fresh breeze. . . . In the background were the mountains high as a wall when you stood next to a wall and looked up

—it is only Mailer, and Mailer's past work, that the prose serves in *Tough Guys*: "A beast had me by the throat and its vitals were in my lungs"; "The compensation for misery, self-pity, and despair is that fed enough drinks, the powers of imagination return with force"; "There was always a touch of hyena in her catlike sumptuousness—a hard, untouchable calculation of the will at the corners of her mouth." The novel contains trials of courage, Irish existentialists, analysis of the orgasms of beautiful women, sly and dangerous homosexual men and, of course, the language just quoted, which could have come from any number of Mailer's essays or novels.

It seems to me that Norman Mailer has searched for thirty years for narrative methods, and for metaphors suitable to his insights and needs. For a time he relied upon what America, and great American writing, provided—Melville, Fitzgerald, and the metaphors in their work, and of course Ernest Hemingway, with whom the younger Mailer was always pleased to compete. But in his vision, in his researchers' pursuits, and in the final writing, Mailer, in *Ancient Evenings*, had the colossal bad luck to find every metaphor and behavior he had sought: "violence, cannibalism, loneliness, insanity, libidinousness, hell, perversion, and mess."

Having sought the outline for so long, what he did when he came to it was simple: he filled it in. This is a dreadful way to speak of a genius and a crucial American writer, but it is probably fair and maybe important to say. *Evenings* did not stretch Mailer toward the psychic frontiers his work had always approached. And Mailer's work has always been about resisting artistic complacency, about the frontiers of both America and art. In fleeing both of those lands, for the comfort (and perhaps flattery) of abstractions about the gods in Egypt, Norman Mailer found the perfect metaphors for which he'd begun to search thirty years before. But he lost the art—he found comfort and a place to rest—which had driven him and his readers for so long.

৵ৡ *MELVILLE'S MAIL* ৶

WHEN HE WAS thirty-three he felt finished. The book he knew to be special—it "is of the horrible texture of a fabric that should be woven of ships' cables & hausers," he wrote; "a Polar wind blows through it, & birds of prey hover over it"—had failed. American and English reviewers had roasted *Moby-Dick* (1851) and in eighteen months the American edition sold 2300 copies. *Pierre* (1852) sold 2030 copies over thirty-five years. It earned Melville the scorn of reviewers—they questioned his sanity as well as his skill—and, by the end of his life, a total of $157.

He had to worry about money, for he farmed a little, but counted on the harvest of his writing, and his wife's small trust fund, for the support of their family. This support was threatened, and since money is a letter from the world to an author about his work, Melville had to face up to the prospect of not getting across his doubting dark vision; for he received too little of the mail that would have assured him that he was heard. As he had complained, in a letter to Hawthorne, in 1851: "Dollars damn me; and the malicious Devil is forever grinning in upon me, holding the door ajar. . . . I shall be worn out and perish, like an old nutmeg grater, grated to pieces by the constant attrition of the wood, that is, the nutmeg. What I feel most moved to write, that is banned—it will not pay. Yet, altogether, write the *other* way I cannot. So the product is a final hash, and all my books are botches."

The well-received author of travel and adventure stories such as *Typee* (1846) and *Mardi* (1849) had become the student of Shakespeare's and Carlyle's works, the hard questioner of heavenly works, and the man whose soul had resonated in response to the works of Nathaniel Hawthorne—"there is the blackness of darkness beyond," he wrote of Hawthorne's tales, and he praised "those short, quick probings at the very axis of reality" which had "dropped germinous seeds into my soul." Melville had lost what ease he'd possessed, and now his work would lose its. Into *Moby-Dick,* which he was writing as he wrote to Hawthorne, he put "the sane madness of vital truth," and the world didn't want to hear it.

And so we come to the exhausted Melville of 1852. He begins to speak—it is nearly impossible, still, for him to be silent—of what obsesses him: the failure of crucial messages to get through, and the condemnations to (or attractions of) silence. Such matters become central; they are the mail of which I speak.

It is likely that Melville had come to love Hawthorne: the handsome older writer, Melville wrote in "Hawthorne and His Mosses" in 1850, "shoots his strong . . . roots into the hot soil of my . . . soul." They were neighbors and saw one another, though less than Melville wished, and then Hawthorne moved away; they corresponded, exchanging books (*Pierre* for *The Blithedale Romance*) and ideas. The case of Agatha Hatch Robertson was relayed by Melville. It involved a young wife who waited seventeen years for word—literally, for mail—from her husband, who had left to seek work. Melville here postulates to Hawthorne how the story of Agatha and her mailbox might be told: "As her hopes gradually decay in her, so does the post itself & the little box decay. The post rots in the ground *at last.* Owing to its being little used—hardly used at all—grass grows rankly about it. *At last* a little bird nests in it. *At last* the post falls" (my italics).

It seems clear that this synopsis speaks for Melville. The story of abandonment and apprehensive waiting for messages is relevant to a writer in Melville's situation—he laments the undelivered incoming mail (the world's attention) and the outgoing mail (his writing) that does not get through. The nesting bird underscores not only the pathos of the disuse of the mailbox, but Melville's sense of his ridiculousness: is he merely a white-stained post? And listen to the rhythm of the repetition of "at last" and "At last" and "At last": it is incantatory, funereal, and about Herman Melville's fatigue.

Melville had steeped himself in Shakespeare's tragedies as he prepared to write *Moby-Dick.* In "Mosses" he had said, "Through the mouths of the dark characters of Hamlet, Timon, Lear, and Iago, he [Shakespeare] craftily says, or sometimes insinuates, the things which we feel to be so terrifically true that it were all but madness for any good man, in his own proper character, to utter or even hint of them."

Whenever he wrote of literature, Melville tended to write about the process of writing in general, and his own in particular; he does so above, homing in on his own relationship to Ahab, who—like Pierre—served as Melville's dark mask. Now he ventriloquized from within his notion of Agatha, and later he would use Claggert and Captain Vere.

It is Hamlet who speaks in the outline of the Agatha story. Grass grows "rankly" around the rotting post; it is Hamlet who, lamenting religious injunctions against suicide, describing life as weary, stale, flat and unprofitable, bemoaning the need for silence ("I must hold my tongue"), calls the world "an unweeded garden" taken over by things "*rank* and gross" (my italics). Melville was low enough in spirit to place himself in Hamlet's garden, and in Agatha's dooryard.

In October 1852 *Putnam's* magazine invited him to contribute work. In December he began to write the Agatha story. Unsurprisingly, he didn't complete it, for he had said its essential elements to Hawthorne; and it was Agatha's situation, not self, that was dark and alive to Melville. She was his emblem more than his story. But he did work at silence and undelivered messages that year, and did give *Putnam's* the tale of *Bartleby*, published in 1853.

The mask through which Melville speaks in the story is that of a decent, pragmatic, elderly Wall Street lawyer (who practices not far from Melville's boyhood neighborhood, and the Custom-House from which he retired in 1885). He is proud to work for robber-barons, he tells us; he is as different from the copyist, or scrivener, Bartleby, as seems possible. And yet, like Bartleby, he is a victim of politics: as he has lost work as Master of Chancery because administrations changed, so Bartleby has lost a position, we learn, for similar reasons. Bartleby comes to haunt the lawyer and his chambers; Turkey and Nippers, matching opposites, strike the motif of doubleness for the story, and it soon becomes clear that something in these opposites, the narrator and his scrivener, is also matched.

For against all wisdom, not to mention sound business practices, Bartleby is kept on, in spite of his refusal to work ("I would prefer not to"), as if the narrator required his presence. It seems that just as Melville finds his mask in the narrator—it is at this time that a campaign of family and friends fails to yield Melville a diplomatic appointment by officials in the new administration of President Franklin Pierce—so the narrator finds *his* darker self in Bartleby. Quite like Bartleby, who ends up dead, "his face towards a high wall," the narrator has chambers on Wall Street that "looked upon the white wall of the interior of a spacious sky-light shaft" at one end, and, at the other, upon "a lofty brick wall." Like Bartleby (who is described, once, as "my fate"), he is in a blind alley of his life, and he looks upon "dead" walls.

In some ways, then, Melville writes not only of existential traps, but of the need to cope with or create or accede to the presence of metaphors of one's interior being. He is speaking of aspects of the consciousness that makes fiction—the creation of alternate, mirroring selves—and it is selfish, needful, cunning, self-pitying and sometimes even generous.

Bartleby, who starved away from an intolerable world—perhaps on behalf of the narrator who had digested too much of it—had been a clerk "in the Dead Letter Office in Washington." His narrator, lamenting Bartleby and humanity, but probably also Herman Melville, speculates on "Dead letters! does it not sound like dead men?" He considers what dead letters might carry—pardon, hope, good tidings—and concludes that "on errands of life, these letters speed to death." For *life*, also read *fiction*.

Published by Harper Brothers into the mid-1850s, Melville also read *Harper's* magazine, renewing his subscription in 1852. And it was in *Harper's* that Charles Dickens' *Bleak House* was published serially in America, from April 1852 to October 1853. There's little reason to doubt that Melville saw those issues, including the issues of June and July 1852 containing the chapters (10 and 11) called "The Law-Writer" and "Our Dear Brother." In them, a man is portrayed so that, for the plot's sake, he might die. He is very much about paper and pen and, like Bartleby (at one point described as "folded up like a huge folio") is a parody of Melville's profession; I suggest that Melville was moved by him indeed.

The law copyist, or scrivener, lives in Cook's Court, near Chancery Lane. (Remember that Bartleby's employer was Master of Chancery and that, well into the mid-twentieth century, America's Wall Street was the equivalent of England's legal Inns.) The man who copies legal documents in *Bleak House*, Melville would have read, calls himself "Nemo, Latin for no one." An advantage cited about Nemo is "that he never wants to sleep"; he is a haunted man. His landlady says, "They say he has sold himself to the Enemy," the Devil; he is "black-humored and gloomy" and lives in a tiny room "nearly black with soot, and grease, and dirt"; his desk is "a wilderness marked with a rain of ink." "No curtain veils the darkness of the night," but Nemo's shutters are drawn; "through the two gaunt holes pierced in them, famine might be staring in. . . ." The filthy, ragged copyist, a figure of total despair, lies dead in his squalid room, the victim of an overdose of opium.

Melville, I suggest, read about Nemo before he wrote his story of Wall Street. He made Nemo his own, though he was drawn to him, I think, because the combination of despair, cruel laws, alienation, copying-out and that "rain of ink" were irresistible. (Note how few writers, especially younger ones, can resist the lures of that tale.) Bartleby turns his face to a dead wall because he cannot tolerate his life. In the Dickens, it is a broken heart, a lost history, a condition in life that is denied by the scrivener. In the Melville, the man who copies dispositions according to common law, the law of human precedent, it is human life itself that is denied. Dickens, when he drew his copyist in *Bleak House*, was angry at conditions in English life; Melville, under Dickens' influence, saw his soul as "grated to pieces" by the great chore of living.

The Encantadas or Enchanted Isles, published in *Putnam's* in 1854, appeals to the contemporary sensibility as much as *Bartleby* or *Benito Cereno*. Although these are long stories, or novellas, they are written for magazine publication and are necessarily concise. The energy that comes of such compression, coupled with Melville's darkening vision and sexual and economic desperation—a third child was born in 1853, a fourth in 1855—results in a fiction that is grim (or effortfully funny, like "The Happy Failure" or "I and My Chimney," also published in 1854), a fiction that appropriates wild symbology from the romance (for example, a tortoise on the back of which is emblazoned a *memento mori*), and the mythic, fablelike qualities one associates with certain contemporary writers.

The Encantadas are the Galapagos Islands, "cinders dumped here and there in an outside city lot," Melville calls them. They are described as a Waste Land in the seas, where natural life is cruel and the human life that drifts in even crueler. Instead of chapters, we have ten sketches; there is no central character, and no single story. The islands become a matrix for authorial consciousness, a repository for attitude and mood. They are metaphors that link Melville's somber music, which describes an island as "tumbled masses of blackish or greenish stuff like the dross of an iron-furnace," yielding "a most Plutonian sight." This is a suite about hell, the outer, physical hell that is analogue to a sad man's interior hell—that, say, of the man who had, in discussing *Moby-Dick,* mentioned "the hell-fire in which the whole book is broiled." These sketches, from the former travel- and adventure-writer, offer a Swiftian scorning song about men who are more like dogs, and about islands that are more like ideas. If there is anyone heroic or admirable, it is Hunilla, of Sketch Eighth, who, abandoned on an island, endures her husband's and brother's death, and years of torture, to be seen, at the story's end, riding "upon a small gray ass . . ." and eying "the jointed workings of the beast's armorial cross." When Melville, the unbeliever, finds a character heroic, that character is often Christlike, and is crucified with rapidity.

It is noteworthy that in describing an apocalyptically ugly wilderness like the Encantadas, Melville called them "cinders" and described them as a waste product of industry. Like all sensitive men and women of his time, and as a former sailor and a farmer, he was aware of the cruel encroachments of industrial process upon the countryside. His *Harper's* story of 1855, "The Tartarus of Maids," is often read as an attack upon nineteenth-century industrial despoliations. It is that, surely. But it is equally concerned with sexuality, and with fiction, and is as much about isolation and long silence as *The Encantadas.*

The stories of this period, when examined in their collection, *The Piazza Tales* (1856), abound in vertical images, phallic shapes—lightning rods, masts, chimneys and the high building that houses "The Paradise of Bachelors" in the story that was published along with "The Tartarus of Maids." As characters in *Bartleby* were paired, the two stories here are paired, the Pickwickian "Bachelors," the Dantean "Maids." The number *nine*—does Melville think of the Ninth Circle of Hell?—is echoed in each: nine carefree bachelors dine, and paper production in "Maids" takes nine minutes. We might remember that the nine months of gestation were significant to Melville at around this time.

So, in "Bachelors," the men dine at the top of a high building in London. They eat and drink in great quantity, are courtly to one another, and are "a band of brothers," with "no wives or children to give an anxious thought." Melville is stating his dream of freedom from the domestic responsibilities that stalk him (and which he cannot easily meet); he also expresses his desire to be free of the sexuality that, his fiction demonstrates, he copes with uneasily: it is Apollonian youth, or bachelor brothers, who most please his personae. Here, the men take snuff together from a silver goat's horn; they remove the snuff, which they will stuff into themselves, by "inserting . . . thumb and forefinger into its mouth." Melville goes to some length to create images that have to do with orifices and infantile pleasure. The bachelors are boys, and their aim is self-gratification, which exists in opposition to the cycles of biology represented in "The Tartarus of Maids," a story that's a matching opposite to "The Paradise of Bachelors," and another Melville tale of the Underworld.

To enter that story's world, one enters a woman's body at her loins— the "Dantean gateway" at "the Black Notch" in a "Plutonian" hollow called "the Devil's Dungeon" that leads to "Blood River." Melville employs gothic images of ruined and decaying structures past which we are led to a paper mill. So we are dealing with female biology, male fear of it, hell, gothic terror and paper.

Our narrator tells us that he is a "seedsman," that when the seeds he mails out are in paper folded into envelopes—he has come to buy more paper—the packets of seeds "assume not a little the appearance of business-letters ready for the mail." And we are back to letters, dead letters, the fiction that constitutes Melville's correspondence with the world.

The story starts out in whiteness, the menacing whiteness of Moby Dick, for all is white vapor, the snow of January, the white walls of the mill, the paper itself. In a factory scene that Kafka might have envied and that Dickens could have written, the narrator confronts this sight: "At rows of blank-looking counters sat rows of blank-looking girls, with blank, white folders in their blank hands, all blankly folding blank paper." It is an industrial nightmare, and a writer's nightmare—especially if he is compelled to write because of inner need, or economics, or both.

If the writer thinks of the mailing-out of seeds as, at once, an artistic need, an economic coercion, an expense of spirit and an invitation to the production of babies who whip the cycle of responsibility round again, he might at this point tie the paper and seed images to the sexual toils he escaped in "Paradise" and slunk through at the Eve's opening of "Tartarus." Melville does. In the very next paragraph we get "some huge frame of ponderous iron, with a vertical thing like a piston periodically rising and falling upon a heavy wooden block. Before it—

its tame minister—stood a tall girl, feeding the iron animal with half-quires of rose-hued notepaper. . . ."

Thus, animal or biological pistoning—the act of sex itself—and the ceaseless sexual cycle our narrator (and Melville) cower before, becomes an "iron animal," a force that cannot be resisted—and it is a product of nature and of thinking man. The paper it prints bears a wreath of roses, like the frightening birthmark on the pink cheek in Hawthorne's story. Cruel scythes cut paper (as cruel saws have made stumps of the trees in the valley), paper pulp is a white river suspiciously sperm- and egglike as it flows into a room "stifling with a strange, bloodlike abdominal heat."

In the confusion of biology and writer's imagination, writer's need and domestic requirements, in the final room of the production process (it is presided over, as if a delivery room, by a woman who was a nurse), the narrator speculates about what could come to be written on all the blank paper he sees. These ruminations evoke those of the narrator of *Bartleby*, for he considers "love-letters, marriage certificates, bills of divorce, registers of births, death-warrants": much, in other words, that might have been on Melville's mind; these documents are the skeleton of what he works at. And then the narrator cites Locke and his comparison of the human mind at birth to a blank sheet of paper—at which point the writer is not only harassed bread-winner, but a mother as well, since his writings are babies as much as babies become the world's blank paper to be scribbled upon.

"Time presses me," the seedsman puns as he leaves: it makes him jump to its bony tune, but it also writes his history upon his own soul. He speaks as all men—the "Ah, humanity!" of *Bartleby*—and as the writer, printed upon even as he imprints his inventions on paper, wraps his seeds (both art and life) and mails them out, hoping for mail in response.

If these are stories of the interior Melville, perhaps the triumph of this period is *Benito Cereno* (1855), a story that is very much about externalities—or seems to be. Like *Bartleby*, *Benito Cereno* excites great writing by Melville, and, like *Bartleby*, it suggests that the obvious is really enigma.

It is 1799, and an American merchantman, commanded by Captain Delano, lies near an island off Chile. The sea is "gray," the swells "lead," the sky "gray"; the "gray" fowl fly through "troubled gray vapors," and the scene is summarized by "Shadows present, foreshadowing shadows to come." So the reader is alerted that he will have to read this world and interpret the grays. He is further warned that what he sees are shadows; what casts them is hidden, and the reader must peer: the story is an exercise in, and an essay about, dramatic irony. As much as the subject is slavery and revolution, it is also perception and invention; it is about fiction, the successes and failures and tactics of which are very much on Melville's mind.

Delano is described from the start as having a "singularly undistrustful good-nature," and is virtually incapable of "the imputation of malign evil in man." From the start, Melville wants us to know that Delano misreads the world. So he resorts to the language of gothic romance. The slave ship looks like a "monastery after a thunder storm"; figures aboard her resemble "Black Friars pacing the cloisters"; the vessel is reminiscent of "superannuated Italian palaces" and her galleries evoke "tenantless balconies hung over the sea as if it were the grand Venetian canal." Delano is placed among the settings in which virgins are pursued by fright-figures, and he should be at home—for he is, in terms of the evil and cruelty that Melville wishes to note, quite virginal.

Gothic conventions not only easily signal fright—we may perceive them; Delano cannot—but can serve to remind us at every turn that dying Europe, the worst of it, encounters the most naive and imperceptive rawness of the New World. Apocalyptic thoughts bring out the best in Melville, who swims in them as in the sea. So we have such poetry about a ship as "while, like mourning weeds, dark festoons of sea-grass slimily swept to and fro . . . with every hearse-like roll of the hull."

Messages do not get through. And so Delano, maddeningly, scarily, cannot overcome his racism and innocence and see past the virtual *tableaux-vivants* arranged for his benefit by the rebel slaves under Babo. The clues that strike us at once are misinterpreted in multiples by Delano. And then the awful symbol, in a story rife with symbols— puzzling rope knots, razors at throat—is uncovered. The ship's figure-head is revealed to be a human skeleton, that of a partner in the slave ship. And we are warned by Melville that what seem to be *only* symbols may be representations of what's actual, that language carries a cargo of the real, and that fiction is a matter of life and death.

The story slips without faltering into another convention, the "true" document that creates verisimilitude (as in the case of Captain Gulliver's deposition or, closer to home, Poe's "MS. Found in a Bottle," or Hawthorne's "discovery" of *The Scarlet Letter* manuscript). The statement by Benito Cereno, a seeming transcript, gives the European account of the slave rebellion, suggests to us how complicated and multifold any actuality is—how difficult to comprehend or relate—and serves to supply small, shuddery details. So we see, for example, that the original figurehead had been a wooden Christopher Columbus; the discoverer (as he was then thought to be, of course) of the New World is replaced by the Old World's grinning corpse: slavery becomes the emblem of an inescapable fact—that we are haunted by our past, that the New Eden is not free of the old evils, that, as Melville complained to Hawthorne, "the malicious Devil is forever grinning in upon me."

A brief third section follows Cereno's testimony. It contains warnings inferred by Melville (and so many others) concerning the social conditions that will ignite the Civil War. It also offers another, a larger and historical, way of examining the events of the story. And it reminds us how, throughout the first part, we saw menace between the slave Babo and his master (then prisoner) Cereno, while Delano saw affection. Delano saw mastery, and we saw captivity. When Benito Cereno's "symbol of despotic command" is examined, it is seen not to be a sword, "but ghost of one," its scabbard "artificially stiffened." Melville does not, I think, speak here only of command, but of men seen as joined by affection who are later revealed to be acting in reversal of their customary relationships (the more powerful obeys, the slave commands). Melville joins notions of political power and emotional liaison, and not only to warn us that slaves rise up. The metaphor works in reverse as well, I think, and we are instructed that lovers are slaves and masters, that men can be unmanned by love (the limp scabbard), and can, as in the case of wan Don Cereno, even die of it.

The warning note is sounded again as Delano points to a sky he names as "blue," but which Cereno cannot acknowledge; to him, it is the gray, perhaps, of the story's opening. The shadows of that early passage are pointed at again as Delano says, "You are saved: what has cast such a shadow upon you?" Cereno answers, "The negro," and so warns a society of its sin and then its price—only then are we told of the empty scabbard—and points as well to Babo, who took Cereno's soul in partial payment for his freedom. The shadow is national, cultural and also particular: Cereno dies, as did his partner.

Babo is the genius of the story—compare his invention, his gift for creating a shipwide fiction, to Delano's good dullness—and his head, "that hive of subtlety," is taken from his body. It is his brain the white men fear. He is further reduced by this barbarism, and yet he becomes more of a threat. He stares at the white man from the post on which his head is impaled. He stares at the Old World and the New Eden, at unmanned Cereno, at church and monastery, story-teller and reader. And he stares them down. He began as a man and became a curse. And *his* message, for some, gets through.

And now we need to move ahead, through Melville's writing and nonwriting lifetime. Hawthorne, whom Melville loved and lost, has risen. He is America's second-most-powerful diplomat, the consul to Liverpool. (He was also Franklin Pierce's Bowdoin friend, and the author of his campaign biography.) Melville, failing at his novels and his efforts to achieve diplomatic appointment, suffering physically, his novel *Israel Potter* (1855) having been launched to sink, contracts for *The Confidence Man* having been signed, was sent in 1856, with his father-in-law's money, on a sea voyage that might bring him back to health and ease. He went to Liverpool, where he visited Hawthorne, who noted that Melville said he had "pretty much made up his mind to be annihilated." It is possible that Melville meant that he was faithless and was reconciled to a death with no afterlife. It is also possible to read the statement as a premonition of death. And it is not difficult, given Melville's state of mind, and his choked-off relationship with Hawthorne, to read the statement as a threat of suicide.

We might keep the possibility in mind as we move ahead to Melville's acceptance, in 1866, of a post at the Port of New York Custom-House at Gansevoort Street, not far from his birthplace. In Boston and Salem, Hawthorne had begun his career at such a place; Melville would conclude his here. But he wrote his Civil War poems, and he went on to write the long poem *Clarel*, and, probably between the time of his retirement as a customs inspector in 1885 and his death in 1891, he worked on a poem that became the ballad "Billy in the Darbies" ("Billy in Irons") that sparked a short novel—it concludes with the ballad and began as a headnote to it—that we know as *Billy Budd, Sailor (An Inside Narrative)*.

We know a good deal about the composition of the novel because of the heroic work of Harrison Hayford and Merton M. Sealts, Jr. They show us, for example, that Melville worked through stages of imagining. First, there was the poem, about a sailor who was to be hanged for plotting a mutiny. Then came Melville's further interest in Billy in the context of the eighteenth-century British navy's concern with mutiny as a threat to fleetwide order. Claggert, Billy's nemesis, was born in further reworkings and then was made more complex, as is true of Captain Vere. The more Melville worked at this (apparent) first fiction in years, the more he thought about the nature of fiction, and the more he sought to deepen (and darken) his characters.

Surely, he did mean much of the allegorizing that readers in the classroom parade before one another. Billy, impressed from the merchant, *Rights-of-Man*, does, after all, cry out "good-bye to you too, old *Rights-of-Man*." Vere does, after all, stand for verity. Billy, as he is hanged, does die as sun shoots through clouds to create "a soft glory as of the fleece of the Lamb of God seen in mystical vision." Melville does liken Claggert to Satan ("the scorpion for which the creator alone is responsible"). And he does liken Billy much to Adam as well as to Christ. Vere, who we are told cannot help but enforce the laws, must hang Billy for killing Claggert, even if the punishment is not fair—for it is just. Billy blesses Vere, we are reminded as we are told that *Billy Budd* is Melville's fiction of reconciliation: left unfinished at his death, it is there to tell us that Melville has accepted fate's cruelty and his own cruel fate.

I would suggest, however, that the novel sustains Melville's preoccupation with fiction, that it creates dark characters for his sane madness, and that he is equally concerned with the mail getting through, and with his participation, to whatever degree, in a suicide.

Melville was a stern and difficult father and, when he wrote, he was removed, cranky, impatient and selfish. We know little of his particular relationship with his son Malcolm, who in 1867 was eighteen years old. We do know that Malcolm was his firstborn, and that he owned a pistol. Roistering one night after work at an insurance office run by his uncle's brother-in-law, he returned home very late, and didn't emerge from his room the next day. That evening, Melville forced the door to find that his son was dead. He had shot himself in the temple—an accident, the Melvilles insisted. What part the troubled father and husband played, or thought he played, in the suicide we cannot know.

But if we read *Billy Budd* with suicide and parental guilt in mind, and in just proportion, interesting considerations arise. Dansker, the voice of insight among the characters in the novel, calls him *Baby*

Budd. The Mutiny Act, which necessitates Billy's death, is described as "War's child," which "takes after the father." In the next chapter, Captain Vere is described as "old enough to have been Billy's father." And so, when Billy goes to his death crying, "God Bless Captain Vere!" it is as if a father is exculpated by a son whom, because of man's laws and God's dispositions, he is required to sentence to death. It is possible that some of the electricity of the Vere-Budd relationship is the result of the father-son analogy that subconsciously galvanized Melville into writing the novel.

In this, another tale of shipboard levels of and kinds of perception, Melville is again obsessed with silence, as well as with ways of telling the truth. Billy, "under sudden provocation of strong heart-feeling," stutters "or even worse." The "even worse" is his choked agony of silence when, falsely accused by Claggert, he cannot speak and, lashing out, kills his accuser. It is silence that leads to Billy's death, and it is silence—the failure of mail to get through—that still haunts Melville. I see little reconciliation here. He still quarrels with silence, and— remember the serpent "for which the creator alone is responsible"— he still quarrels with God.

But Melville too is a creator. He thinks hard of that for which he's responsible. So in chapter 2 he worries about the form and function of his art, discussing Billy—"he is not presented as a conventional hero"—and his story, which "is no romance." He is speaking of what's actual, I think he says here, not of the symbolic. His subject, he tells us, really is death and silence and inexorable laws. In chapter 11, making Claggert an Iago, he worries that he errs in the direction of the gothic, or that his reader will, and he discusses "realism" and "Radcliffian romance." Chapter 13 reminds us that profound passion can be enacted "among the beggars and rakers of the garbage"; he is worrying about the effectiveness of his writing tactics, the ways of fiction are very much on his mind. In chapter 28, toward the novel's end (and his), he all but declaims or apologizes: "Truth uncompromisingly told will have its ragged edges; hence the conclusion of such a narration is apt to be less finished than an architectural finial." As he writes about Billy and Captain Vere and Claggert and Dansker, he writes about how he writes.

In 1851 Melville wrote to Hawthorne that "I have come to regard this matter of Fame as the most transparent of all vanities." Now, thirty years and more later, writing of Vere's end, he may speak of his deepest self: "The spirit that . . . may yet have indulged in the most secret of all passions, ambition, never attained to the fulness of fame." But I do not think he meant widespread notice to be his primary aim, any more than he meant riches when he complained about the earnings from his work. He was speaking, I would submit, about the ways in which the world could demonstrate to Melville—to any writer— that his work had been read and that it had made some difference. He was speaking of most earnest correspondence.

And there is Melville, who wants the mail to go out and to be delivered as much as he wants to receive it. He is riding in the stagecoach that carries the mail. At way station after way station, horses are changed, coaches are changed, the freight and mail and passengers roll on toward the end of the day. Melville writes to Hawthorne: "Lord, when shall we be done changing?" He sighs, in the corner of the stagecoach, in the corner of his life, "Ah, it's a long stage, and no inn in sight, and night coming, and the body cold."

✑ ISLANDS, ICEBERGS, ✑
SHIPS BENEATH
THE SEA

A KEY WEST conch collector named Bra Saunders told Hemingway
a story about a sunken Spanish liner; Hemingway made the story his
own in "After the Storm," published first in *Cosmopolitan* in 1932, then
in his 1933 collection, *Winner Take Nothing.* When the collection is discussed, "After the Storm" usually isn't. And yet that story does matter,
and not only because it reminds us of Hemingway's Key West days of
drunken fishing trips, boxing exhibitions and rifle-shooting shows. In
it, Hemingway created a prose new to him (and sufficiently distant
from his contemporaries for them to overlook it). He formed the persona of Harry Morgan, who would be consciously developed in "One
Trip Across" (*Cosmopolitan*, 1934), the "The Tradesman's Return"
(*Esquire*, 1936), and finally in the book knitted together from these
stories, seams showing, as the 1937 novel *To Have and Have Not.* And
he created an image which surfaced from the sea off Key West and the
sea of John Hawkes's dreamings to finally float on the fictive surface—
what Hawkes called a "mirage of imminent departure over the lip of
the earth"—as a metaphor crucial to Hawkes's work.

To Have and Have Not is full of hoked-up social engagement and lit-
erariness, and it is not a good book. Its protagonist, Harry Morgan,
who fights for the independent life of his family, and who loses his life
in fighting to retain his sense of self—a constant preoccupation, that
salvation, in the Hemingway of the thirties—is not a well-made character. He is poses and stances, a one-man scrapbook of hardihood.

He ostensibly shows us his thoughts, but they all too frequently are speeches:

> They all double cross each other. They sell each other out. They get what they deserve. The hell with their revolutions. All I got to do is make a living for my family and I can't do that. Then he tells me about his revolution. The hell with his revolution.

It's not bad; but it's simply exposition disguised as thought, and it cannot stand up to the language of "After the Storm," from which the novel—at least its brutal tone and brutalized persona—quite probably grew. The interior monologue above could, allowing for diction, have been written in the nineteenth century. Compare it to "After the Storm," written as anecdote or interior monologue:

> Well, I went out of there and there were plenty of them with him and some came out after me and I made a turn and was down by the docks and I met a fellow and he said somebody killed a man up the street.

One might at first be struck by the incantatory "and," which Hemingway had used before. Under the influence of Joyce, and with particular admiration for the consciousness streaming through Molly Bloom, Hemingway chants "and" in *To Have:* ". . . if I lie here all night and can't sleep I'll go crazy and if I take too much of that damned stuff I'll feel awfully all day tomorrow and then sometimes it won't put you to sleep and anyway I'll be cross and nervous and feel frightful." But each "and" connects another integer of thought, another topic of concern; the sum of the topics is simply a magnification of the weight of any one of the topics: the effect is of breaking down "four" (restlessness, anxiety) to say "one and one and one and one" (restlessness, anxiety: nothing gained).

But in the passage quoted from "After the Storm" we are told no thoughts—there's very little thinking in the story. It is a story about what happens to people in a crushing world, and the prose is a catalogue of where the body is, where it goes, what it does. The passage from *To Have* is a complete sentence which, despite its rhythms evocative of the chant of the mind singing to itself, in fact does convey, traditionally, a whole thought. But the sentence from "After the Storm" conveys no thought; it conveys an entire *act*. The mind of the voice in the story exists only in terms of what happens, not (until the very end) what it reflects about what happens. The story, I am suggesting, is told in a prose which in turn tells how the mind of the story responds—it sees the world in terms of event: it is anticontemplative.

Each of six uses of "and" in the sentence from "Storm" connects happening to happening, not thought to thought. So we learn that, to the protagonist, a complete perception is made up of flight, pursuit, further flight, then information: the whole is more than the sum of its parts; a "complete thought" is in fact the shape of an event as the protagonist records it.

Such a prose is crucial to the world created in "After the Storm." This world is not congenial to contemplation, for it is a world of randomness and cruelty. The story begins with a fight which "wasn't about anything": the world of the story is one in which a man may be strangled, and another sliced with a knife, over no issue except "something about making punch." In a world so lacking in design, people react without plan or pondering. And so the prose is not designed according to sentences, which form the heart of the structure of thought-out telling.

This prose of action is, like the environment from which it erupts, eruptive. One action, performed in response to a basic stimulus— fear, anger, self-defense, wanting—leads to another action, *causes* another action: "The biggest boat I ever saw in my life laying there and I went along the whole length of her and then I went over and anchored and I had the skiff on the deck forward and I shoved it down into the water and sculled over. . . ." There is no causality in the story's world except that of the event immediately preceding. One event occurs because the prior one did; there is no logic, only sequence.

The prose tells us this. It shows the character to be prodded by what happens, makes him a creature of sequential action. As Marie Morgan learns in *To Have*, "You just get dead like most people are most of the time. I guess that's how it is all right. I guess that's just about what happens to you." What happens to the original, unnamed Harry Morgan in "After the Storm" is that he is driven in flight from the consequences of the bar fight out to sea. He comes upon a ship, wrecked in a storm and sunk in shallow water and he fights, underwater, his nose bleeding from the pressure, to break into the ship. He fails to do so, is driven away by a storm, and learns that "the Greeks had blown her open and cleaned her out. . . . They stripped her clean." He thinks, at the end, for the first time, saying of the Greeks, "They picked her clean. First there was the birds [who picked the corpses of the drowned], then me, then the Greeks, and even the birds got more out of her than I did."

The protagonist himself, then, is little more than a carrion-eater. And at the end of the story he suggests the only unity available in the disorderly world of the story—the pecking order of creatures who feed on the dead. His whining conclusion is far more faithful to the sort of man Hemingway suggests Morgan to be in *To Have*, by the way, than the mock-heroics he actually implants toward the end of that novel. In shaping the book, Hemingway was stitching together pieces—the separate stories—not working from a whole vision. He makes Morgan's brave end not in response to who Morgan is, but to what a Hemingway hero should be. In effect, Hemingway turned critic, studied his canon, and wrote what Hemingway would write *if* he were making a tapestry, and not a crazy quilt.

There is no description in all of *To Have* which is as powerful as this one in "After the Storm":

> I could see her rounded over and she looked a mile long under the water. She was lying on a clear white bank of sand and the spar was a sort of foremast or some sort of tackle that slanted out of water the way she was laying on her side. Her bow wasn't very far under. I could stand on the letters of her name on her bow and my head was just out of water. But the nearest port hole was twelve feet down. I could just reach it with the grains pole and I tried to break it with that but I couldn't. The glass was too stout. So I sculled back to the boat and got a wrench and lashed it to the end of the grains pole and I couldn't break it. There I was looking down through the glass at that liner with everything in her and I was the first one to her and I couldn't get into her. She must have had five million dollars worth in her.
>
> . . . I could hold on for a second to the edge of the port hole [after diving to it] and I could see in and there was a woman inside with her hair floating plain and I hit the glass twice with the wrench hard and I heard the noise clink in my ears but it wouldn't break and I had to come up.
>
> . . . I could see the woman floated in the water through the glass. Her hair was tied close to her head and it floated all out in the water. I could see the rings on one of her hands. She was right

up close to the port hole and I hit the glass twice and I didn't even crack it.

Under the water, his nose bleeding, his head aching, his strength gone, the narrator sees the other world (that of those who "have," in *To Have*) and he cannot get through to it. The ferocity with which he tries to invade the sunken ship suggests the symbolic importance of his action. But the action isn't symbolic to him; he sees no symbols: he sees something he wants and tries to achieve it. The world of wealth, the world—this is more important—which he simply *wants*, no matter why, is unattainable. It is a dreamworld, a world of the dead. He is damned to mere consciousness and to his meager pursuit of nothing more than safety and desires he cannot comprehend. He leaves the ship and its floating corpse. Later, decades later, the ship is visited by a writer whose protagonist gets in.

Forty-two years after the appearance of "After the Storm," John Hawkes writes this in his 1974 novel, *Death, Sleep & the Traveler*: "When the divers descend and open up this unfortunate ship, I thought, they will find all the drunken passengers packed in confetti and paper streamers tangled like dead rainbows. The ship will be rusting, but the travelers will still be packed together in silent joy. All of them will be preserved in kelp and seaweed and bright paper."

Writing of his "marvelous mythical cousin" who took him for walks on the New England coast when he was a child, Hawkes describes the abandoned house she took him to—"a monstrous castle-like hull of a house"*—and, speaking of possible sources for his story "The Nearest Cemetery," and for *Second Skin,* which came from the same wellspring, Hawkes says, "the abandoned house she used to take me to is clearly the source of three related visions or images that have obsessed me as long as I can recall: the abandoned light house, the abandoned ocean-liner leaning on its side in low tide far from shore, and the New England fishing village on an island."

While speaking at Colgate University in 1973, trying to cite sources for his imagery—in response to one of those dreadful questions about just how fiction gets written—Hawkes told his audience that "in some story by Hemingway" there is an image of a sunken ship, looming like

---

* "Notes on Writing a Novel," *Brown Alumni Monthly* (January 1973), 73–74.

an underwater city, which fascinated him. There's little doubt that he was referring to "After the Storm." And whether he has been referring to the story directly, or to the childhood image, Hawkes has been evoking a version of that sunken ship for a long time and in remarkably various ways.

In his short first novel, *Charivari* (1949), Hawkes suggests the ship figure, although he doesn't offer it directly. In this novel of sexual terror and dream states, no one does anything directly. In the coastal town to which Henry has fled from marriage (whether actually or mentally), he notices this harbor scene: "Sailors from Madagascar, ships from the Caribbean, the Puritan, iron hulks from Liverpool, plunging their crimson sails and tarred lines through the surf, they hovered in the harbor." This same surf is the vehicle of death from which a drowned woman is fished (as are so many deaths, fetal or adult, fished up in Hawkes's fictions—from the fetus of *The Beetle Leg* to the narrator of *The Blood Oranges*). And water is a carrier of death again in *Charivari*, when the husband of the woman who makes Emily's bridal gown awakens to see "the unfinished, fluttering, wedding gown"; as if the gown is on a drowned corpse like the one in Hemingway's story, "A green light filled the room with the depth of the sea." If, in this novel of topsy-turvy perspectives, the sea can fill the houses on shore, so can the shipwreck be lifted from the ocean and plunked onto land: "They passed a windowless trolley car, warped and grey, covered with bits of rusted wire and surrounded by glittering bits of broken glass, that lay overturned in a vacant field."

The abandoned New England house of his childhood walk, and abandoned houses of all other sorts, become combined for Hawkes, with the sunken ship, as an image of death and of love reversed, and of the impingement by the past on the present. And so the grotto in *The Blood Oranges* with its chastity belt, the wrecked bomber in *The Lime Twig*, the ruined motel in *The Innocent Party*, the empty white house in which Allert ponders in *Death, Sleep & the Traveler*, the sinking khaki bus in *The Blood Oranges*, the wrecked homes under tons of water in *The Beetle Leg*, the emptied insane asylum in *The Cannibal* (or, far more striking, the empty movie theater in which the same film is shown again and again to no one)—all are variations and permutations of the "abandoned ocean-liner leaning on its side in low tide far from shore."

Although there is no ocean liner in *The Blood Oranges*, there is a boat being launched down a too-narrow street; the street through which the boat is dragged to the sea is lubricated with blood. Not only is the image of a bloody birth, it is presided over by an old man resembling a goatish god, "his obviously unspent passion . . . hanging down and rotating loosely like a tongue of flame." Lust and birth are combined so that there is a sense of the cycle of love, and of love's insatiability. But the boat is a white boat and it is watched by the protagonist Cyril and the woman who blames him for her husband's death; as Cyril tries to argue against the presence of death, or time, in his artistic creation, a life eternal through visions of art, the woman he is trying to persuade of death's absence joins him in seeing a white boat launched. As surely as Cyril's vision falls apart, that white boat is a signal that it is bound to fall apart.

For in Hawkes's preceding novel, *Second Skin*, another white boat appears menacingly, the lifeboat in which Tremlow and his fellow deserters rape Skipper, the novel's narrator. Skipper, too, tries to argue for permanence in a world of change, for the attainability of a vision which permits psychic survival from wars and domestic terror. But he ends up enduring pain and failure, carrying his *memento mori*, his photograph of the *U.S.S. Starfish*, on which he was raped. As events begin to pull him into that rape, he opens his porthole and looks down: "there was nothing to see except the golden water, the paste of foam, the passing schools of bright fish, the shadow of the ship sliding down to the deep. And all the while overhead there was a stealthy clamor around the white lifeboat." As the violence mounts, Skipper describes himself as "hanging on tightly to the moonlit ship though she was still, flat in the water like a melting iceberg." And as he is being raped, Skipper notices that he has been pushed into the bottom of the white lifeboat. He is rescued by the ship's chaplain, who hauls him up a rope as the lifeboat falls into the sea.

Whenever Hawkes uses a variation of the boat image, or its synthesis with the image of the deserted house or lighthouse, he is creating an island. The island of the ship's lifeboat is a dystopia, to be balanced by the utopia of Skipper's "wandering island." The stag party in the inn, of *Charivari*, or the beach scene in which the corpse is found, or the scene in the dressmaker's house, or that in which Emily descends inside herself at the end of the novel—each, washed by the same tide which surrounds that sunken ship, is a psychic island on which Hawkes's character is marooned. When in *Blood Oranges* Cyril tries to create a paradise in Illyria, he must pay penance by visiting the grotto in which the chastity belt is kept—in a castle on an island to which the characters wade. And each island is one of reversal—not only of time or expectation, but of love and sexuality. In the loveless world of the protagonist of "After the Storm," not only riches but a dead woman float just out of reach. What is desired and what is dead—they are simultaneous in the Hawkes and Hemingway images.

Of the cousin who took him for coastal walks Hawkes writes, "surely she must have been my first love." Later he says, "I would be terrified and more in love with my cousin than ever." And then he writes of the cousin, "She embodied what I've feared and yearned for ever since." It would be fruitless to say much here about sublimations of love that kill the adored and make her safely attainable as image, as the mourned and cherished. We have said this for years about Poe and Hawthorne and James and Hemingway, but once we have said so, we have failed to learn more than the mere fact—that it is possible that a process of sublimation, loving safely those who are safely dead, has gone on.

The point, rather, is to say that Hawkes *uses* these psychic islands to create strong metaphoric effects, and that his fiction writhes with the dreaming dead. In his "Notes on Writing a Novel," Hawkes describes his "personal waking dream" of the underwater ship:

> I stand alone at the edge of a straight empty shore at low tide and gaze with both fear and longing at an enormous black derelict or damaged ocean liner that looms in awful silence in knee-deep water about a mile from shore. A few lifeboats hang halfway down the side of the ship from their davits; on the ship there is no movement, only the black immensity and the smokeless funnels and the occasional small flash of some piece of metal on the deck or in the rigging. And then I am compelled to walk slowly but deliberately into the muddy shallow water and toward the ship.
>
> In this waking dream I know that I am going to have to walk the entire distance from shore to the listing ship. I know that I am going to climb somehow to the tilted deck of the abandoned ship. I know that I must discover its vast world, must pry open some metal door rusted half ajar and enter the ship until I discover what it contains—either its treasure, if childhood hopes prevail, or its emptiness, its floating corpses.

Hawkes says, before he offers this description, "my vision of the ocean liner hasn't appeared as such in my fiction." But the ship finally

does appear, Hawkes's vision is finally rendered fully, in *Death, Sleep &
the Traveler*. And the similarity of ship images in *Death* to the image
in Hawkes's "Notes," as well as his possible regret (in 1973) over not
yet having used the image fictively, at least suggest that he wanted
to use—consciously, tactically—that vision which had for so long
used him.

It is evident that *Death* continued Hawkes's concern for antimo-
nogamous love. In fact, the New Directions catalogue described
Hawkes's *Travesty*, as the completion of his "trilogy." And so it is fair
to say that Hawkes was consciously pursuing a design, in *The Blood
Oranges, Death*, and *Travesty;* he was carefully manipulating his customary animal imagery, the locales absent from our maps, the over-
turnings of our expectations of sexual behavior; he was reversing assumptions about the separateness of dream states from waking, and he
was creating some very exciting prose.

A part of this latter pursuit seems to be the image of the abandoned
ship. Allert, the protagonist, menace, full-time pornographer and
part-time victim, as well as narrator of *Death*, is forced by his wife Ursula, part of a *ménage à trois* with Peter, a psychiatrist, to take an ocean
cruise. On the voyage he meets Ariane, innocent and Siren at once,
a creature of pornographic proportions in her sexual energies, the
bitch-goddess of adolescent imaginings (the cousin was "marvelous"
and "mythical"). Allert murders her, is tried and acquitted. Ursula
leaves him and, like Skipper, Allert survives, denying nothingness. It is
a novel in which a man descends into himself—the book abounds in
images of plunging into swimming pools, into the sea, into sleep—toward his most essential being. The voyage is toward death, it is a daring of death.

In *Death* more than Hawkes's concerns come together, whether as a
result of Hawkes's own study of his works, or the unconscious pushing
through to the surface of all his motifs simultaneously. His abandoned
ship appears more strongly and directly than ever before. In "Notes,"
Hawkes says his obsessive vision "is one of potential and desolation. It
suggests the undiminished power of childhood experience, it defines
what I'm most interested in writing about."

There is no child in *Death*, although the image suggesting the
power of childhood experience is central. It is possible to see Allert as
in some ways the child of Ursula, Peter and even Ariane at times; and
he does recollect his childhood thrill at posing before his mother's

mirror in a pair of women's panties: they fit him "like a second skin,"
Allert recalls. And Hawkes in "Notes" recalls of Skipper that the personal vision of the ship "becomes suddenly literal in *Second Skin* when
Skipper happens to see a long dark ship drifting by on the horizon and
finds himself filled with both joy and dread." So in *Second Skin* Hawkes
refers to his vision, and in *Death* Hawkes refers to *Second Skin*. It is as
if he were trying to pull together strands spun over twenty-five years of
writing.

The same possibly conscious effort is more apparent when we consider the ship Hawkes creates in *Death*. Allert is "lying bulky and
naked in a strange bed, tasting the salt and feeling the stasis of the ship
in my own large body." The ship is "high and sharp and clear, a paint-
smelling flowered mirage of imminent departure." He leans forward,
"looking down, watching as the lights, which ran the entire length of
the ship, began to disintegrate and sink." Later, Allert describes the
ship as plunging "like an abandoned freighter." At the time of Ariane's
murder—she is thrown overboard much as Skipper was plunged toward the sea—Allert says, "And then along the entire length of that
bitter ship I saw the lights sliding and blurring beneath the waves. . . .
I saw the ship's fading lighted silhouette beneath the waves." And then
finally there is Allert's vision of the ship, which merges that of Hemingway and Hawkes, as rusting beneath the sea, the travelers still
packed together in silent joy.

Death, Sleep & the Traveler is a very good book, though for me it cannot match *Second Skin*, in design, in characterization, even—splendid
as the language often is—in prose. But why, when all Hawkes's themes
and images converge, is the novel not his best? Of course, we are
speaking here of taste. And I want to hasten to add that I do not believe
Hawkes can write a book which doesn't possess some of the most
original writing of our time. But I do think there is a problem here,
and that it is more than a matter of my admittedly partisan devotion to
Hawkes's early works. The problem seems to speak to the larger issue
of how fiction works.

What *Death, Sleep & the Traveler* reveals is an archetype come from
its generating, structuring depths to the surface. In this novel, Hawkes's
original personal vision has become a present reality to him, part of his
own (consciously observed) interior landscape. When he tries to use
the vision directly, instead of metaphorically, it becomes *too* direct. It is
now like an iceberg on the surface, rather than the mostly submerged

ice mountain of which the iceberg once was a part. It was Hemingway who said, speaking of undisclosed elements in fiction, that "the dignity of movement of an iceberg is due to only one-eighth of it being above water."

Shocking as much of the imagery in *Death* is, and brilliantly written, nowhere in that novel does the abandoned-ship image work as delicately or as powerfully as in the scene in *Second Skin* where Skipper as child, locked out of the bathroom by his suicidal father, tries to pry the door open, and pry his father from death, by wooing him with his cello playing. Here is the "treasure" opposed to the "corpses," which Hawkes says in "Notes" is the dynamic generated by the image of the ship. The scene is so moving because something domestic and tangible is at stake. The ship image is the generating force behind the metaphoric island of the locked bathroom (or the one in which Skipper desperately makes music). A metaphor emerges, and the potential horror or delight offered simultaneously by the ship image, according to Hawkes, is created from beneath the surface.

But in *Death*, the vision which generated metaphor, and its dynamic of terror-delight, has broken away from the heavy mass of the unconscious and has floated off on its own, high on the surface, a *subject* in its own right. When archetype rises to the surface it can become superficial. In *Death* it is used as an outer representation of an inner fearfulness which really cannot proclaim itself except on inner terms—except, that is, in terms of metaphor. But there is no metaphor created by the ship; there is the ship, crucial to Hawkes, scary (at best) to us, making no metaphoric displacement in the water because it rides so high.

In *Death*, the ship on top of the psychic sea, and the fictive one as well, loses its mystery and its generative force. Nevertheless, it does work well on outer, public (if customary) terms. It is the gothic presence of death, it is the presence of the past, an emblem of Allert's (and Hawkes's) daring to plumb the self. However, tradition has trained us to see gothic images in narrow ways when they are on the surface. In effect, the boat in *Death* becomes a version of the gothic haunted house; it does not resonate (as other permutations of the ship image do resonate) beyond itself, suggesting vast depths.

When Hawkes is at his most powerful, his personal visions create public images—lighthouses, abandoned buildings, tin coffins floating in the ooze of melted ice—which become psychic islands. The best

Hawkes fiction creates a rhythm of hope, or pursuit, and a counter-point avoidance. Characters move toward and away from each other's imaginary personal universe. Each lives on an island and each island is in some way a metaphor which is perhaps generated by Hawkes's own profound personal image evocative of "potential and desolation."

In a response to a paper given in November 1973 at Stanford's conference on "The Creative Process in Literature and the Arts,"* Hawkes speaks again of his cousin, disclosing that she is only a few years older than he—not far older, as he thought when he was a boy—and she and Hawkes have "had a lengthy argument about detachment by mail." Hawkes recounts their trips to the deserted house by the sea, describes the first trip there as "a fabulous moment, and in some way sexual." He then says, as if he were explaining the effect of his abandoned-ship image on his fiction, and not discussing memory and mail, that his cousin "says that detachment is an abomination in the lives we lead, and I insist that detachment is the only way that we're able to live or create anything. She says that one must be committed and that detachment means indifference." Hawkes replies to her, he says, that detachment "is a psychic state that one learns in the face of the most overwhelming emotional destructiveness. You can live and create only when you manage to control, to keep at a distance the terrors that exist within the human being." The last line of Hawkes's reply is "At any rate, artists all depend on detachment."

He is probably right. For Hawkes and Hawkes's fiction, he clearly is. He writes, in a John Hawkes reader called *Humors of Blood & Skin* (New Directions, 1984), of his 1976 novel *Travesty,* calling the short book "an account of the privileged man's own brief excursion into adultery." It is really Hawkes's response to Camus's *The Fall,* and a brilliant meditation on art and time—"a comic novel," Hawkes calls it in *Humors,* "about the fatal importance of the imagination." Here, Hawkes's obsessive imagery becomes part, once more, of the underpinnings of story, surfacing only occasionally and serving the narrative instead of demanding its service. So we read of "these small islands created out of haste, pain, death, crudeness . . ." and an abandoned farmhouse with its "windowless wall of an old and now roofless barn built lovingly, long ago, of great stones from the field."

---

*Richard Yarborough, "Hawkes's *Second Skin," Mosaic* 8, 1 (Fall 1974), 65–75. Hawkes's reply begins on p. 73.

Similarly, the image works as image—hence with force—in the 1979 *The Passion Artist,* parts of which recall the asylum so wonderfully made in Hawkes's early *The Cannibal.* Konrad Vost stumbles through a marsh and comes upon the "crumbling remains of the old mill . . . a high partial wall of jagged stones and a great iron wheel rusted into the antithesis of motion." He comes upon a naked bather, as well, and he is the cause of her death. As if he had drawn back from contemplation of that childhood vision, and then had been called to it again, Hawkes here reunites the ruins and water, death and sexuality.

And in *Virginie, Her Two Lives* (1982), on the trail of de Sade, and in pursuit of what he calls in *Humors* the "similarity between the pornographer and the lyric poet," Hawkes generates his obsessive imagery inside his protagonist ("Rivers were running within me," she says) and creates a stark chapel dedicated to sensual considerations. Virginie sees "our chateau as if from without and afar: the gates bearing their incomplete designs of ivy, the walls the color of dark sand, in one corner the single low tower that was plump to my eye and roofed in its gently sloping cone of black slate." While the ruins and the waters and the dreaming state are not always central to *Virginie,* they are not far off.

As if distanced for a while, they return, at least in parts of Hawkes's newest novel, *Adventures in the Alaskan Skin Trade.* In *Humors,* Hawkes describes this book as "intended to be as autobiographical as I can make it." And here is the ship of Hawkes's dreams again, "our dark ship making its slow way out of the dawn," in a darkness "that shrouds black reefs, uninhabited shores, wrecks at sea." The *Alaska,* carrying our protagonist, blasts its whistle to shatter a looming iceberg. The sound causes the heroine to think, "We were inside the sound, inside some terrible gathering of lighthouses with fog horns chorusing all together. . . . Ships might have been colliding all around us; catastrophe was booming." Sunny dreams of standing before "a ghostly mountain of ice lying dead in our path." Her Uncle Jake picks her up and "he dangled me over the side so that I could wave to the Indians"—as Skipper, in *Second Skin,* hung over the side. "My little skull was a lighthouse," Sunny remembers dreaming. And when she wakes, "I slipped to my knees in my top bunk and pressed my face and chest to the porthole, a wave crested, unfurled and flung itself against the glass. . . . Again we wallowed, the porthole was again submerged."

Here, Hawkes's protagonist becomes the image that so impressed itself upon Hawkes from Hemingway's "After the Storm": the un-attainable woman, underwater, behind the porthole. John Hawkes, studying his life, perhaps studies his art as well, an art of wandering islands and cities beneath the sea. As he always has served, so Hawkes here takes the point on a dangerous foray. It is easy for a novelist to confuse his dreams and visions with what he writes in response to those visions. Hemingway did so. *To Have and Have Not* and *Across the River and Into the Trees* are the result. John Hawkes now faces the danger he has faced throughout a distinguished career—of tapping his usual psychic resources, of using his usual dreams, of relying upon his usual metaphors, and therefore of risking the loss of new language, new fictive worlds.

I am an avowed admirer of John Hawkes, and think his lyrical prose some of the loveliest our fiction can offer. I am, too, sympathetic to his sufferings at the hands of reviewers—his fate in the marketplace in general—and I go so far as to sorrow over his considerable praise from academics, the WE to whom I earlier referred, because I fear that they seek to encourage Hawkes to write what is "teachable" and teachably "post-Modern," what is neatest for *their* purposes, not his.

Hawkes, like every writer who taps his inner imagery, must determine when he is to avoid his own urgings and the temptation to use what becomes a habitual vocabulary of images. I write of Hawkes at such length and in such detail not only because I admire him as writer and man, but because he is exemplary now—a first-rate writer, in the vanguard of American fiction, facing the need with which every writer sooner or later must contend: the need to turn his back on what has nourished him over nearly thirty years of fiction writing, or the need to reexamine, at least, the ways in which he will make use of those psychic islands—and dangerous icebergs—that have served him so well for so long. This is an essay, then, in wishing well.

·٤ξ EVEN THE SMALLEST ε٥·
POSITION

As UNEMPLOYED Americans of our time cry for jobs, good books out of print cry for republication. Some are louder than others. Some of the unemployed we notice more because of their dignity and our sense—it grows as we consider them—that our own transactions are diminished without their participation.

Such a book is Leslie Epstein's *The Steinway Quintet: Plus Four,* which was allowed to go out of print before most of us knew it existed.* We are lessened by its absence from the marketplace. Provoked by my experience of reading it, and by its unavailability to most readers, I invite your attention here to bodies that float like blimps, the Angel of Death on the Lower East Side of Manhattan, the murder of the Jews of Europe, and the making of music in Vienna by Gustav Mahler. For all this, at once, is the stuff of the title story of Mr. Epstein's book.

"The Steinway Quintet," like all good stories, is about what we have and don't want, what we want and don't have, and what we don't want to know we do and don't have. Since the story is an advertisement for a job, I dedicate my essay on this unjustly ignored work to the politicians—in publishing, in Washington and in the classroom—who help to make *job* rhyme with *Job,* and to whom out-of-print books are leftover goods.

After being rejected by the *New Yorker* and *Esquire,* "The Steinway Quintet" was initially published in 1976 by *Antaeus.* Following its ap-

*While I wrote this essay, Leslie Epstein wrote two more novellas about the hero of "The Steinway Quintet." These three stories were published, as *Goldkorn Tales,* in 1985, and were monumentally misperceived and misrepresented in the *New York Times Book Review.* But Leib lives.

pearance there, the story was selected for Martha Foley's *Best American Short Stories of 1977* and became the title story of a book published by Little, Brown. But the print run was only fifteen hundred books (of which, the author thinks, half were sold) and every book was mistakenly bound without the last page; extant copies contain a glued-in final page in a typeface different from that of the rest of the text. By the end of 1977 or early in 1978, the publishers remaindered the book (i.e., sold off the unsold copies), and it has since been unavailable. The author's literary agent had arranged for Epstein to receive fifty copies, which were boxed and left in a corridor for pickup by the mail service. The janitorial service picked them up instead, and they floated that night, with exhausted facial tissues and unwanted correspondence, as incinerator smoke above the skyline of Manhattan. It is not always easy, as so many people are learning these days, to be of use to the world.

Yet nothing Epstein writes is inconsequential. He is able to offer humor and cataclysm—at once; lyric and epic concerns—at once; your individual heart and all of my Europe or America—at once; cold precise description of the blood's hot rush—at once. From his first novel, *P. D. Kimerakov*, through *The Steinway Quintet* stories and *King of the Jews* (which I would suggest to be a major novel for our time) to *Regina*, his latest novel, Epstein has been ample and brave. Who else has dared to write funny lines about the Holocaust? And he's a master of that peculiar form, not a novel and not a short story (*Don't call them novellas!* cried Katherine Ann Porter, who wrote them so well): the long story. "The Steinway Quintet" is a splendid example of that form's richness.

Listen to its opening lines: "Good evening, my name is L. Goldkorn and my specialty is woodwind instruments, the oboe, the clarinet, the bassoon, and the flute." The narration is Goldkorn; the story is a voice. As a musician, Goldkorn tells you his name and his instrument in one sentence: he is what he plays; his job is who he is; Goldkorn is his work. Note, too, that he is speaking directly to you about his essence. Be warned: you are responsible for intimate news, and he is vulnerable and charming. He not only wants you to know something, he wants you to *do* something, to feel something, maybe to yield something up. Great fiction shows us all fiction, in certain ways. Goldkorn is a voice-of-fiction, and he knows you are there. He has politely addressed you. Like his clarinet or flute, his story is an instrument.

Goldkorn—like all the narrators on wonderful pages who have pulled the reader up close enough to smell the warmth of their skin—Goldkorn is after results.

Listen, now, to the early paragraphs of the story:

> Good evening, my name is L. Goldkorn and my specialty is woodwind instruments, the oboe, the clarinet, the bassoon, and the flute. However, in 1963, on Amsterdam Avenue, my flute was stolen from me by a person I had not seen before, nor do I now own any other instrument of the woodwind classification. This is the reason I play at the Steinway Restaurant the piano, and not clarinet, on which I am still proficient, or flute, with which my career began at the Orchester der Wiener Staatsoper. Examples of my work on the latter instrument may be found on recordings of the NBC Orchestra, A. Toscanini conducting, especially the last movement of the Mendelssohn-Bartholdy Fourth Symphony, in which exists, for the flute, a wonderful solo passage.
>
> I wish to say that I am an American citizen since 1943. My wife is living, too. These days she spends most of her time in bed, or on the sofa, watching the television; it is rare that her health allows her to walk down the four flights of stairs that it takes to the street. In our lives we have not been blessed with children. Although the flute was in a case, and the case was securely under my arm, a black man took it from me and at once ran away. It was a gift to me from the combined faculty of the Akademie für Musik und Darstellende Kunst, when I was fourteen. Only a boy.

See how his days and health as well as his wife (whom he does love) come second; first comes his art. For this is a story about art and artists in an age of enormities. It is not a reflexive, "metafictional" story told by itself about its writing or its author; there is subject matter and a high regard for—a long and crafty gaze upon—the world of people just as dopey and spectacular as you and I. But it is also about the art on which Goldkorn does, or tries to, thrive.

As he makes his history and his domestic life, his work and love and much of his plight, known to us in a very few lines—they are not mere information, the sort of brand-name stuff that second-rate writers think of as convincing details—we realize that how Goldkorn gives the data tells us who he is. As he tells us his past, he returns to the violence, street crime in this case, that surrounds his life (and yours) as it informs his exposition. But remember the tender "Only a boy" that occurs at the end of his reminiscent second paragraph: it is the lyric note sustained in the story, the soft-petaled flower that lives where street dogs trot.

The story begins, and we are in the Steinway Restaurant on New York City's Lower East Side. The musicians, waiters and customers— nearly all of European-Jewish extraction—are playing or listening to minor music. But the players take their work and themselves seriously, for they are musicians and, like Goldkorn, they live their art. Listen, as he describes the restaurant's atmosphere, to Leib Goldkorn creating silence with sound:

> Salpeter picked up his bow. Murmelstein, also a violinist, put his instrument under his chin. Also present were Tartakower, a flautist, and the old 'cellist, A. Baer. For an instant there was silence. I mean not only from the Steinway Quintet, which had not yet started to play, but from the restaurant occupants, who ceased conversation, who stopped chewing food; silence also from Margolies, Mosk, Ellenbogen, still as statues, with napkins over their arms. You could not see in or out of the panes of the window, because the warmth had created a mist. Around each chandelier was a circle of electrical light. Outside, on Rivington Street, on Allen Street, wet tires of cars made a sound: *shhh!* Salpeter dipped one shoulder forward and drew his bow over the strings.

It is, for an instant, the cultured and elegant Old World. The story's epigraph is from Shakespeare's *The Tempest*, also about magic and art, which is set on an island, away from the world, the better to make the magic happen and the better to make us accept it. The restaurant is such an island too—"You could not see in or out. . . . on Allen Street, wet tires of cars made a sound: *shhh!*" Even rude intrusions of the coarse world become the audience at a concert as it hushes itself, *shhh!*

Goldkorn and the others live within the magic (or needs, or zaniness: what you will) of their vision. They see *their* way. So when two men walk in, they are described (erroneously, we soon learn) as "a tall Sephardic Jew and a short Jew, also of Iberian background." They are seen as such because the see-ers receive the world in their terms, terms of "mister Sigmund Romberg's *The Student Prince*," "roast duck and Roumanian cracklings," and, naturally, glasses of hot tea. Even when the two tough guys make their move, the watchers see that "both Sephardim were holding big guns." Deaf Mr. Baer, unaware, keeps playing the cello. One of the toughs breaks his bow, demanding (and achieving) silence. Baer remonstrates. The tough jumps on the cello and shatters it.

A protest is raised: "'I am an American citizen since nineteen forty-three' some person cried. The voice was familiar. It was certainly that of Leib Goldkorn." Thus, he inserts himself more directly into the historical parts of his narration, but in such a way—such a marvelous way—that he is his character while he is his narrator, as he addresses us months after these events took place. After the naive exclamations and further savageries (when the cook is pistol-whipped, the musician Goldkorn asks us, "Is this not in many ways an act as terrible as the destruction of a violoncello?") only *then* does someone say, "Friends, these two are not Jews." At last they realize that two Puerto Ricans swallowing amphetamines are holding up the restaurant. The world has invaded their littler world of small magic, their eccentric vision. And much of the rest of the story will demonstrate the contest be-tween what practical people tell us the world really is, and the spell under which Goldkorn and his companions wish—probably need—to live.

At this point, Goldkorn breaks off—there is a chapter break on the printed page. He returns with

> Greetings! L. Goldkorn once again. I have paused for some time.
> It was necessary to mix medicaments for my wife. Now she is
> sleeping, my life's companion, with no obstruction of nasal pas-
> sages. Sweetly. Also, it is sometimes desirable to settle the nerves.
> I am too old to speak of such terrible things, the destruction of
> property, attacks to the head, without becoming myself upset. This
> is to explain the presence of Yugoslavian schnapps. Alcohol is good
> for you; it allows to breathe the hundreds of veins which surround
> the heart.

This will be the structure of the telling—his present plight seen in the context of his history. We will read in two times at once. We will expe-rience story-telling as a necessary journey to the past—necessary for Goldkorn to take, necessary for him to force or lure us into taking. And we will see that he stalls by breaking off; he temporizes because, while he wants to be in his past, for whatever needs and practical purposes, he also does *not*, periodically, want to be there himself. He does not wish to face the actualities of the invasion of his dreamy life by the Hispanic holdup men. He has learned that invasion's lesson and he shies from recalling the truth of cruelty in the world.

Ishmael, telling us *Moby-Dick*, did the same. *Moby-Dick* is a recollection and performance by a survivor. Like Coleridge's Ancient Mariner and Pip in Dickens's *Great Expectations*, the narrator of "The Steinway Quintet" is also a survivor, condemned to wander restlessly and to tell his urgent tale. Goldkorn evades the telling at least momentarily, as does Ishmael. Goldkorn runs to his wife or his schnapps. Ishmael flees to long diversions about whaling. But, as the whaling chapters become increasingly metaphoric, mirroring Ishmael's apocalyptic concerns, so Goldkorn's evasions are also futile. He must return to the tale. And we see another truth about story-telling: just as the artist seeks to persuade us, often against our will, and for his own ends, so he must labor against his own will. Narrative history in sentences may be a sentence that the story-teller serves. The tellers may even be said to serve a function by serving such communal sentences on our behalf. Perhaps that is their job. They will require payment from us.

As Goldkorn now recounts the life of V. V. Stutchkoff, the Steinway's owner, we hear again the common story of the life of much transplanted European Jewry, including the story's first reference to the obvious—the Nazi eradication of the Jews. The point is important, for as we see Goldkorn's present life and past adventure simultaneously, each informing the other, we will also see the Holocaust informing events at the Steinway.

Stutchkoff, hearing the commotion of the holdup, slowly—he is tremendously fat—hauls his great weight upstairs to the dining room from his office. "It seemed as if there would be no end of him," Goldkorn prophetically says, describing how the huge form deliberately rose and rose into sight. Frightened, amazed, finally threatened, the bandits fire away as Stutchkoff, like a magic being, ascends. They kill him, plunder the register, and try to make their escape, but the back door is locked, and they cannot flee through the front door because Stutchkoff's great corpse is blocking it. Police sirens approach.

Now that the world has invaded the magical island of these marvelous characters' collective imagination—Epstein is so like Chekhov in rendering collective states of mind—the curtains close over again. We are once more away, on the island of *The Tempest*, in the province of

Leib Goldkorn's vision. One character rages about sewing on a yellow star, and we remember the Holocaust, and why these people see aspects of their lives in certain inescapable ways. Stutchkoff's wife kneels to untie her husband's shoes and necktie—it is a duty of the orthodox Jew—so that the soul may fly up. At once, there is a differing opinion: someone suggests that she does her duty so that the Angel of Death will not be tempted to linger. (Meanwhile, a diner, who has introduced himself as a Freudian analyst, declares, "She is undoing the knots that might hinder the release of . . . his *anima*. It's Jungian psychology." Epstein's wry humor glows with life, in the presence of death, as a profession is put on its guard, a state of mind satirized, and a character drawn—all in three sentences.)

There is, of course, rabbinical debate among the Jews. To live, among them, is to endlessly discuss. Margolies offers Zev Wulf of Zbaragh as his authority on responses to the Angel of Death. Ellenbogen counters by citing the Maggid of Mezritch. The widow ripostes with the Spola Grandfather:

"No, Shmelke of Nikolsburg! The dead man must not see his own spirit depart!"

"Mister Ellenbogen, am I not correct in assuming that the purpose of this action is to prevent the Angel of Death from becoming entrapped in the glass?" [They are covering a mirror.]

"That is a valid interpretation, Mister Margolies."

"Pfui!"

Doctor Fuchs spoke from the viewpoint of science: "I agree with the negative opinion of our friend Mister Mosk. These are Jungian daydreams. A regression to primitive thinking. Even children—"

"Look, gentlemen! She has finished!" It was Salpeter, our first violinist, who was speaking. "Now dear V. V. Stutchkoff, patron of the arts, may depart!"

Every person's eyes swung back to the corpse.

"THIS IS THE POLICE DEPARTMENT SPEAKING. YOU ARE SURROUNDED. COME OUT WITH YOUR HANDS IN THE AIR. YOU MUST SURRENDER."

That voice came from an amplified horn. One of the gangsters, an adolescent, a boy, shouted back:

"We ain't going nowhere! We got hostages! We're cold killers!

You gonna find out, because we going to kill them one by one!" He
threw a blue-colored pill into his mouth. His colleague smiled, and
swallowed a red one.

"Mama!" The cry came from the rear. "Mama!" Martinez, the
cook, raised his bloody head from the floor.

Again Leib falters, and the story breaks. He evades what he knows, but
then he is forced—as artists must perform, as lovers must woo—to
return:

> Hello? Hello? Leib Goldkorn here. What a poor memory! Have
> I mentioned my performance of the *Italienische Symphonie?* Or
> have I not? Only a short time ago I happened to hear this same
> recording on radio station WQXR. The difficult aspect of playing in
> the orchestra of A. Toscanini—of course there were also many
> joys—was tempi, tempi, always the tempi! An artist went as fast as
> he could and—"No, no, no, no: Allegro! Allegro *vivace!*" The key
> to the final movement, this thrilling passage, is breath control:
> whether I possessed it or whether I lacked it you will judge for
> yourself.
>
> Now the radio is off; this is because of the television for the
> entertainment of my wife. She is watching from the sofa, with her
> medicaments on the table. A red cotton nightdress and a white
> cap: adorable, the little mouse! You will pardon me? I am sipping
> hot milk with hot coffee. No sugars. I am fond of sugars. However,
> Clara has diabetes. I think now we are having a spring morning.
> The tree on the street has birds in it and the buds of leaves. The
> clouds are not serious clouds. I have suffered since February from
> a disturbance in sleeping. A result of the events in the Steinway
> Restaurant? A sign of advancing age? Brandy from plums is good
> for this condition. Yes, but the bottle is nearly empty. An inch at
> the bottom is all that remains.

Notice how Goldkorn's thoughts insist upon running together, as in
the second sentence of the story and, again, in the paragraphs I've just
quoted. He experiences a great deal simultaneously; his life, hard as it
was, cannot be easy now. His style tells us this. He is his voice, and in
small ways he reveals—probably because he wants to—that he is afire
within.

Now: the heat is turned off, the restaurant is embattled, the crooks are frightened and high on pills, and soon they are full of liquor. They are holding rich Jews captive, they think:

"Oh, sure, you wanna have a little drink!" the youth opened the *fine champagne* and filled to the brim a tall highball glass. "So, Mister Weinberg, Steinberg, Feinberg! You wanna drink to one hundred thousand dollars?"

"Ha! Ha! Ha! Weinstein, Feinstein, Steinstein! Ha! Ha! Ha!" The tall man, the man with the successful moustache, slapped the face of his younger colleague. "Names of Jews!"

"Ha! Ha! Listen, Mister Greenberg—"

"Mister Goldberg!"

"Ha, ha! Drink it down!"

Only once before in my life, thirty-two years in the past, have I tasted a liquor of this class. The Hispano-Americans continued to slap one another. They each swallowed a pill. They put more of the cognac into my glass.

"My name is L. Goldkorn, specialist in—"

"Ha! Ha! Ha! We gonna get a hundred thousand American dollars!"

The temperature falls, and so does the snow, and the night passes. Goldkorn recalls—his vision controls him, remember—the snow having blown from right to left (like Hebrew writing). "Then that night, in some respects no different from any other, came to an end," he remembers. He reminds us of the Passover *seder* question, "Why is this night different from any other night?" The *seder* commemorates the passing of the Angel of Death beyond the doors of the Jews in their Captivity. Their lives are somehow informed by captivity. And their funny debates on responses to corpses and the Angel of Death might suddenly strike one as more than funny, though never, in Epstein's story, as less.

The police send Spanish-speaking negotiators to lure the crooks out. To resist, they command the Steinway Quintet to drown out the police by playing. It is a savage scene. The quintet plays the *Can-Can* while Baer, in shock, moves his arms, as if to play, but with nothing held within them. And then the quintet plays the *Barcarole* while the tall thug, Jesus, considers the rape of the woman who, at the story's beginning, had requested "Some Enchanted Evening." The story is about enchantments—naive ones, artistic ones, drugged and criminal

ones, and even enchantments with America. The rape is about to begin. Goldkorn thinks:

> *Here the poorest boy may rise to the highest position in the nation.*
> *Many have done so: many more will do so in the years to come.* From
> what source, and from what distant time, had this thought come to
> my mind? At once I knew. These were the words of Judge Solomon
> Gitlitz, spoken to me, as they have been spoken to thousands of
> others, upon the occasion of my American naturalization. I stopped
> playing Offenbach then. I stood up on my feet. Murmelstein,
> nearby, pulled my clothing:
> "Don't make trouble. Sit. Sit down."

But the enchanted, innocent immigrant from Europe's latter hells says,
"Listen, young man, you must not do this. You have a fine tenor voice."
And we must laugh, or decide not to cry. Goldkorn goes on: "What
were the possibilities of such a situation? I tapped the shoulder of her
attacker, who slowly turned toward me his head: 'You are dragging the
flag of your country in the dust.'" The rape is beginning:

> I heard gasping. Behind my back Jesus had risen on all fours. The
> foot of the woman had lost a shoe. It was at this point not possible
> to look longer. "Young man, one thing more. My dream . . . was to
> ride on a tramcar. These went through the streets of Vienna,
> throwing out sparks, and each was equipped with a musical bell. If
> you work hard, if you learn to speak American English, you will be
> able to ride in a silver airship. I guarantee this to you! We have a
> land of opportunity! Do not commit this terrible crime. Stop your
> colleague! It is nearly too late!"
> "Oh! Oh! Oh!"
> The second shoe of the lady was gone. Each of her legs was now
> forced into the air. What happened next was that Leib Goldkorn, I
> myself, had knocked the hat of the tall Puerto Rican off his head
> onto the floor. Not only that; violently I was pulling his hair. Suc-
> cess! The man rolled aside, and the lady—she was missing her
> collar of pearls—began to adjust her purple dress.

The rapist and his partner are outraged. And we hear the old, the familiar, refrain. "The Jew is going to die." And: "Going to die: All Jew."
So we learn a lesson about the courage of this artist and about heroes—remember that Leib Goldkorn tried to forestall Jesus, at first,

by telling him stories about his, Goldkorn's, life: he is always the tale-teller—and we learn that the world colludes, strangely enough, in creating the enchantment we thought to be exclusive to the people of the Steinway Restaurant. The world speaks in the voice of these people's history—"Going to die! All Jew."—and Goldkorn (and we) are learning a hated lesson. In the context of the story, Goldkorn is the enchanted party; we, the readers, his audience, are of the world. So we listen, now, not only because we are learning about Leib Goldkorn; we are, reluctantly, learning about—and perhaps also denying—what might be aspects of the world, and therefore of *us*. We are not Goldkorn the narrator. We are the ear in which he whispers. Yet, might we not wish to become like silly Leib, who acted so bravely? Especially if it means that we aren't a party to what the world threatens him with? The story makes it difficult for us to be neutral, no matter how alien these enchanted Jews might be to our lives. Can a story make us Jews, and artists, and victims of a frightening world? V. V. Stutchkoff's corpse begins to answer these questions by turning "warm and some-what maroon" while a patron, a Jew, as if in Europe in the thirties, pro-tests that he isn't a Jew, but a Greek, and begs to leave. (He reinforces his Greekness by crying out in what he takes to be Greek: "Bazouki!" he will cry, "Metaxa!") The corpse's bulk before the door keeps him from it. And Goldkorn once more, on the page of his story, turns away.

When he returns, he is drunker, more disturbed by his present life and his memories of the past. He says, "Of the events of three months ago I shall speak no longer. Why should I continue? What more do you want to know? There are not any surprises. How could there be sur-prises when I am here, alive, a survivor, speaking to you. The suspense element is gone." Like every artist who performs, Goldkorn knows his audience in advance and feels forced to emulate them, in self-defense, by speaking as his harshest critic. Perhaps representing Epstein's wor-ries during composition, but surely Goldkorn's own, Leib bemoans the fact that the crucial life-and-death note, the cornerstone of sus-pense—Will Our Hero Survive?—is sacrificed by the convention of first-person narration that only the living address us. But the com-plaint also tells us that more than breathing is at stake here. How breathing—quite literally *breathing*—is accomplished, as we shall see, is one of the story's crucial concerns. So, Goldkorn whines, he can't continue. So you dutifully beg him to go on—as he wanted you to. Please, you say, it *isn't* boring, I'm enthralled. And, having heard what each artist craves, he relents. Like the voice in Beckett's *The Unnamable,* "in the silence you don't know, you must go on, I can't go on, I'll go on." He does. And so does the enchanted lunar world of the Steinway Restaurant:

> "All things get worse," remarked once Sigmund Freud, who lived at Berggasse 19, only a few blocks from my boyhood home; "they don't get better." Of course the famous alienist was referring to the condition of living persons, but at the Steinway Restaurant, on Wednesday afternoon, it applied to dead people, too. By this I mean the corpse of Vivian Stutchkoff, which now unmistakably smelled. It was not hot in the room, although it had grown uncomfortably warm. The problem was the airlessness. Not a fresh breath came to us from the world outside. The smoke of Tartakower's, and others', cigarettes hung in layers over our heads. And with every inhalation, even when done through the mouth, came the smell of—it is difficult to put the experience of one sense into the language of another: it was a thick, sweet smell, and a tangy smell, too. Like boots, partly, and partly like caraway seeds.
>
> "He stinks!" said Mosk, the Lithuanian waiter. "P U!"
>
> Also, he was for some reason swelling. Large already, an impressive man, Stutchkoff had begun to bulge even further—not dramatically, not all at once, but steadily, like bread that is rising. By two o'clock his buttons were straining, and several had burst. But perhaps the most painful of these transformations was the way in which his skin altered its color. It had been, that morning, pink and rosy as if through some miracle he had been frozen alive. Think of the pain for Hildegard Stutchkoff, seated nearby at the window, as that complexion deepened to purple and then turned an absinthe green.

And the analogy to the European Jews' experience also continues— they were criticized for not resisting the Nazis, perhaps with stiff dead babies in their arms instead of guns. Murmelstein, crazy with fear, begs the corpse of the legendary boss to help him. One of the bandits calls:

> "No talking! Talking not allowed! This is dead individuals! Talking to ghost? Ghost? Ha-ha-ha! No such thing! Ain't spirits! Jew! Listen! Ain't anything! Ain't anything! Ain't anything!" With the

gun in his hand, Jesus was striking Murmelstein, a parent, on the back of his head.

"Hey, cut it out!"

"You are striking a trained musician!"

"No! No blows on the head!"

The staff of the Steinway Restaurant had become agitated. Someone restrained the hoodlum's arm. Someone else—this is true, I am an eyewitness—began to strike him upon the hip. Let people say what they wish; let them even deny it. We acted, friends! At that hour we fought them back!

At this point—note how much shorter the intervals have become—Leib, his stamina failing, breaks for psychic cover once again. He returns to speak more directly about his wife:

> Clara is not well, after all. I thought it was the croup but she is making a sound as though she meant to bring up her phlegm. There is also incontinence of the bowels. We treat this as a little joke between us, but if I dared, if it were not undistinguished, I would request that she wear rubber pants. Am I not speaking of a disgraceful human condition? What a scandal! And what is the point? Tell me! She does not even know that she is alive! "Am I living or dying?" she said. A better way to treat old people would be to kill them. Kill them off would be better! There is no mind in her. No mind left! . . . Already it is growing quite dark. But where was I? Yes, I remember. I would accept any employment in the woodwind area, if necessary even the saxophone. In the percussion group I have at times played the piano. Is that something you already know?

And, now, he has revealed his primary purpose—he is asking for work, for what was once called "a place." He seeks a place as an artist, and probably in other terms too; he is a man displaced in life by life itself. While the HELP WANTED columns of newspapers advertise available jobs, I, when I was unemployed, and millions of Americans unemployed at this moment, and probably Leib Goldkorn too, would claim that the advertisements of we who seek a place would properly be labeled HELP WANTED. Leib calls upon us for this help.

In a long, beautifully understated scene, the Steinway Quintet turns on the spotlight, assembles near the piano, and plays Viennese music in honor of Stutchkoff. They respond to the general dark, and to their light, and to themselves. Leib plays Tartakower's flute. Listen:

> As our program continued, this feeling of closeness—better to say an absence of division, of divisiveness—grew to include those with whom I was playing: Murmelstein, Tartakower, A. Baer, Salpeter. It was as if the Steinway Quintet were a single person, giving a solo performance, as if invisible threads bound us one to another, so that when Salpeter moved his arm upward I felt myself pulled ever so slightly in his direction. And at last there grew to be a similar bond with those who were listening below. We could at that time hardly see them—only the shine from a pair of eyeglasses, a white shirt collar, the napkin on Margolies' arm. Like heads bobbing in an ocean of darkness. Then I felt myself to be not this Leib Gold-korn, no longer the separate citizen, but also a part of that ocean, like a grain of salt, no different from those other grains, Mosk, or Ellenbogen, or the woman, Hildegard Stutchkoff, or the lifeless corpse of her husband, yes, even—do not be alarmed by what I now say—even the two murderers, for they were a part of that ocean, too. That ocean. That darkness, friends. We know what it is, do we not?

The music bridges the ocean as Prospero's magic reaches over the ocean to and from *The Tempest*'s enchanted island. Leib Goldkorn is not alone as, perhaps, for instance, now and then, the story-teller is not alone when he is doing his job.

There are many curses in this story—that of brutality and hatred and bigotry; that of the losses to the erosions of time; and that of *self*. The curse of self, as Goldkorn shows us, is the artist's curse. See how pleased and even surprised he is by the connectedness he feels, if only for a moment. We, of course, begin a conversation with Leib Goldkorn at this instant, if we haven't done so before, by telling him that we are also drowning in self; we know what he means; we envy his connected-ness; we want to feel it too. And suddenly, for the space of, say, a quarter-note, Leslie Epstein connects us—non-Jewish, perhaps, per-haps not habitual appreciators of art, much less artists; perhaps sens-ing that we would not choose to spend much time with this schnappsy, hand-waving, sentence-drifting, dandruffy and liver-spotted man who, with his language, lures and then dodges us, drops and grunts to pick up once more his story's thread. Epstein connects us to this foreign person as nimbly as Ravel's *Bolero* once seduced the boys and girls of more classically innocent days. This, too, on Leslie Epstein's part, is an act of enchantment.

But the world of the Camps is still with us. As at the Camps the captors strip the captives of their clothes, and the people at the Steinway hear, "Get your clothes off! Yids, move your asses!" Leib Goldkorn describes the victims in a familiar way: "All of us, musicians, waiters, patrons, were huddled together, as if on the lip of some common grave. Our bodies in the light of so many bulbs were extremely white. Ghosts of ourselves when clothed."

It is time for magic. The legendary rescuer, former patron, and present corpse, V. V. Stutchkoff, stirs:

> From the open mouth of the restaurateur there now issued a
> thin gray-colored shadow, a mist, a kind of a cloud—impossible to
> know what precisely to call it. Steam perhaps. Perhaps smoke.
> Everyone saw it slowly rising, more and more of it, growing taller,
> spreading outward, almost the size of a person.
> "Ghost!" Chino exclaimed, although in a whisper.
> "*Un diablo!*"

Leslie Epstein's magic recurs: he remains *funny*. Ellenbogen, naked except for his socks and citing the Maggid of Mezritch, turns all the Steinway's chairs upside down, so the corpse's soul won't be tempted to have a seat and stay awhile.

The strange mist rises, descends on all within, then rises again, and all are magically weeping. It is tear gas, of course, thrown in by the police. The floor begins to shake and strange lights descend from the sky. "Angel of Death," the crooks scream. Naked, but with the hidden key to the back door, the captives escape. Leib Goldkorn has fled us and returned, on his narrative's pages, once more. And the magic of the Steinway Restaurant goes on, while Leib anxiously waits for the doctor, whom he has summoned to his wife. As in the story's past the captives flee, this happens:

> What we saw was that between us and the Steinway Restaurant
> the snow was actually rising. It was a whirlwind. At the top of this
> swirling storm, a black shape hung in the air. It neither rose nor
> descended, but simply remained, roaring, in defiance of gravity, of
> physics, of reason itself. From the belly of this form columns of
> light shot downward and played over the surfaces of the snow.

Looking back, Salpeter points toward the door of the Steinway:

> This had swung open. Standing inside it was Vivian Stutchkoff.
> He appeared to be stuck. He backed up, onto the light of the
> chandeliers, then came forward and once again caught in the door-
> frame. It was at this point, naturally, that my own sanity came into
> question. . . .
>   . . . On the third attempt, by turning a few degrees sideways,
> Stutchkoff got through the door. He came then bobbing toward us.
> Our party retreated to the opposite curb. "Golem!" some person
> cried. Margolies and Ellenbogen were rocking in prayer. Still
> Stutchkoff came, enormous in size, rising and falling, skimming the
> snow, like a gas-filled balloon. I barked with laughter again. . . .
>   . . . Stutchkoff, meanwhile, had glided to the center of Rivington
> Street. There he paused, bouncing about, turning left and right;
> then he fell face down into the snow. A tall and a short Puerto
> Rican stood in his place. It had been some kind of trick! Yes! The
> restaurateur had been their shield!

Laws of science and facts made clear seem to explain such miracles
as these. We of course want to know why and how such events can occur. But I think that we're disappointed as much as we're relieved by
unenchanted explanations. We often want to believe in magic. We are,
when we read, children opening the *Arabian Nights,* and we want the
spell to go on, even if it means letting enough of the grown-up world
in, disguised as data, gas, the use of a corpse as a shield, if *that* is what
it takes for Scheherazade to keep talking. This is what fiction rises to;
it disproves the finality of death (the body walks through the door), and
yet it rubs our noses in death's total truth. It is magical and it is mundane, simultaneously. (I should remind you that Charles Dickens, in
Bleak House, has a man explode in a greasy, tallow-smelling puff because of spontaneous combustion caused by the ingestion of a lifetime's overdose of cheap gin. Dickens was so hurt when critics pointed
to the scene as an unscientific flaw in his majestic novel that he came
to believe in his own magic. Rather than revise the scene's impossibility, he came to love it—it is the usual author's cheap trick. When
Bleak House was reprinted, he staked his reputation, in a preface, on
there *of course* being such a phenomenon as spontaneous combustion;
lots of people explode because of gin, leaving their bedrooms empty

except for some grease on the wall and a strange smell, as of underdone mutton. As I have said: in great writing, we find all great writing.)

Goldkorn flees his history, and us, one last time. He returns to bring us up to date on dead musicians, jailed Puerto Ricans, his dying wife. He gives his address and tells us, "I would appreciate knowing of even the smallest position, on any type of musical instrument." The reader is addressed directly: he has the power of a god. As we think of what has unfolded, and then think of the events in our own physical and psychic lives which we are powerless to control, we might realize how we, the gods hearing Goldkorn's prayer, are as powerless as mortals. Affirming such a frightening realization through such a subtly constructed metaphor—it turns one's notions of a god upside down—is no small achievement in a story.

Goldkorn is powerless in every conventional sense. He is desperate for money and is, obviously, out of work. He cannot pay for schnapps or for the doctor. He can never replace the flute, stolen from him in a barbarous world. He admits to drinking too much, and to being insufficiently religious in any orthodox sense. But art, as we know, is magical. So Goldkorn *does* have powers. Art may imitate time, as Goldkorn has done, in his comings and goings, to give us an illusion of hours passing. Art can also shatter time, as Goldkorn has done, by giving us past and present at once. Art can *keep* time, as in the playing of the music of, say, Sigmund Romberg, by old European Jews on the Lower East Side. And art can invent time, as Goldkorn does in returning to his own childhood, and to the time of innocence in the life of civilization—before it, like Leib, fell upon hard times.

"Yet," he says—and it's humankind's ultimate reply to the outer dark—

Yet I am speaking truthfully when I tell you I feel myself to be now the same person who received the gift of a Rudall & Rose many years in the past; and like that young boy I am still filled with amazement that merely by blowing upon such an instrument, and moving one's fingers, a trained person may produce such melodious, such lyrical sounds. You are no doubt aware that with the flute the breath passes over the opening, and not into a mouthpiece, as with other woodwinds. Its music is, therefore, the sound of breathing, of life. It is the most ancient of instruments, and the most basic, too. A boy can make one with a knife and a hollow twig. This is what shepherds did, playing to sheep.

In one of contemporary literature's most life-affirming passages, Leslie Epstein turns a musician's story into music itself. Here, or should I say *somewhere*—for where *is* the book, outside a few hundred libraries, to be found?—here, we have Biblical and Greek lyric; we have a domestic story of a couple in poverty and sore plight on Manhattan's West Side; we have the story of the Camps and the Russian tales and plays of group dilemma. The voice of the story is similar to the voice of prayer nearly anywhere driving home insistently the need of the story-teller to *say*. All of this is present in "The Steinway Quintet": unmistakably a wonderfully authentic, idiosyncratic and individual piece of work.

Goldkorn's voice is his story, and he ends his appearance before us in the guise of a two-thousand-year-old gust of breath. It is the breath of life, then, that begs the world for work. Music and the song of language, in the air or on the page—*life itself*—is looking for a job.

❧ PRACTICAL LOVE ❧

SILICON, and not cholesterol, impedes our blood.

None of us is black, and none is yellow, brown or beige. None of us is crippled or is sick for very long. None of us drives erratically or doesn't drive at all. There isn't one of us who shoplifts, beats a baby, waters the whisky of a friend or cheats at pool. We don't discuss politics. We aren't Moslem, Jew or Catholic. We rarely listen to music, engage in abstract discussions, rape or pillage or loot.

I am playing cards with the fellows. I am hiding from your wrath. Or I am napping when you want me out repairing the roof, cleaning the yard, attending to the lawn grown long. You are a big-busted, long-legged blonde, and what you like to do is shop, cook or gossip with friends during long afternoons. We do not hold each other's flesh. We care about my not getting fired from the job at which I'm hardly competent. We're fretful over the having of babies in general, the handling of our budget in particular, and the fact that, as American Dagwoods and Blondies, promised from birth that our lives would be happy and full, we are simmering under our skins because that promise isn't kept yet.

With exceptions, interesting ones, that is who we are, you and I, according to the authors of twenty-four pieces of fiction in sixteen glossy magazines for September 1983. We are Dagwood and Blondie, Mr and Mrs Rip van Winkle, Ozzie and Harriet, Luci and Desi, all those Mr and Mrs Whatsits in newspaper comics and on radio shows and TV sitcoms: we are the "boys" who go bowling while the "girls" stay home with bridge mix; we are Kate and Petrucchio but have no poetry to say; we're tall, clean, slender, hopeful of wild sex, frightened if it happens;

we are the all-American boy and girl of whom Ernest Hemingway wrote in "The Short, Happy Life of Francis Macomber," published in *Cosmopolitan* in 1936:

> Look at the beggar now, Wilson thought. It's that some of them stay little boys so long, Wilson thought. Sometimes all their lives. Their figures stay boyish when they're fifty. The great American boy-men. Damned strange people.

And he said:

> They are, he thought, the hardest in the world; the hardest, the cruelest, the most predatory and the most attractive and their men have softened or gone to pieces nervously as they have hardened. Or is it that they pick men they can handle?

Hemingway revealed what he feared in himself, and how he saw his countrymen; the editors of *Cosmopolitan* thought that Hemingway's countrymen and countrywomen would like to read such considerations. What about us? Have we changed in our estimate of ourselves? Have our editors?

According to what I have seen, head buzzing with starchy recipes and menstrual cramps and prelubricated condoms, during my most unscientific inspection of who and what it's said we are in the popular fiction of our moment, something like the following seems possible. If women, we are troubled by our lives at home, by our need to flee them. If men, we are either self-employed or "in computers," and our marriage stands on shaky rock—on sliding shale. Our days and nights are circumscribed by cheap meals, the longing for thinner thighs, and better days with worsening kids. The life in our sex life is determined by surveys, and we match our performance, or our torpor, or the needs we daren't speak, or the fears we daren't dream, to tables of how many did or didn't, and what a person called Doctor says it's okay to feel. We are longing to cook for seventeen on a dollar a day in an air raid. We wonder if our living room has personality. We want to know if our marriage can be saved. We are here on the face of the earth to be happy and as good at what we need to do as anyone else who does it too. The new American Manifest Destiny is our guiding principle: we are here to get better; getting better is our right; our magazines tell us how to do so. Our fiction reflects that love of process, that sense of being in possession of know-how, data, technologies, tools, good things for people who want to be best.

Of the sixteen magazines for September 1983 that I read, one was a weekly, the *New Yorker,* and I simply read the issue for September's first week. All would be called "slicks": they are expensively printed on shiny paper; they are successful at reaching enormous numbers of readers; their editors are scientific at selecting what their readers want, I think; and each, from *Vanity Fair* to the *New Yorker* to *Ladies' Home Journal* and *Playgirl,* carries fiction. (The only exception in September was *Ms.*) We can tell the teller by his tale. We can, too, tell something of who the teller (and his editors) think us to be. For these American magazines select fiction with the care they exercise in the picking of sex surveys or diet articles: they want the reader to receive what they have told the reader, for years, he wants to get.

So I read *Playboy* and *Penthouse,* the allegedly revived *Saturday Evening Post,* which will still run an old Louis L'Amour story in which it is said, "What a man wants to find in horses or partners is stayin' quality." On my desk and in my dreams and under my feet and rising like a bright tide were 1,727 pages of Dream Kitchen Filled with Ideas and How I Live with the Pain and Full Tweed Overcoats with a Forties Flavor and Losing Fat with Fiber and How to Keep Housework from Breaking Your Back and When to Talk to Children about Sex and What Makes Sex Better? ("12,000 Couples Share the Secrets of Intimacy," and that is really sharing), and How Love Came Too Late for Jack and Jackie plus Rita Hayworth's Life Story and all the letters Ved Mehta ever received while growing up and when to say "Berlin Alexanderplatz is not outside the norms of film narratives, like the films of Godard's. It is not a meta-film, like Syberberg's *Hitler.*" While the magazines are roughly of a size, their typefaces are different, so they contain significantly different numbers of characters on each page and I could not compare numbers of words. I counted as a page of fiction any page containing any fiction, even when there were pages offering only a few lines, or a single column or paragraph of fiction on a page that carried a good deal more—shirts and car radios (*Esquire*), bosom beauty and *Intercourse Illustrated* (*Playgirl*), free cheese and petite-sized dresses (*Ladies' Home Journal*), salad dressing and cigarettes (*Redbook*), good cartoons (the *New Yorker*) and a poem about hairwash (*Good Housekeeping*). There were 148 pages or fragments of pages of fiction in the 1,727 pages I read. That's about 8 percent. Making allowances for how few of those pages contain only fiction, I'd say that we're dealing with magazines whose content is 5 to 6 percent fiction.

Two of the works of fiction are by foreign authors, but they merited consideration because American editors selected them for American readers. Two of the stories were selected by editors from books of stories about to be published, which means that they read manuscripts of ten-or-so stories; their being in manuscripts ratified by book publishers made the job somewhat easier, I suspect. Five of the "stories" are really excerpts from novels; again, they are ratified before fiction editors see them, and they need not achieve the rightness of form and aptness of rhythm which are at the heart of the story—they meet other needs.

We are, if women, profoundly disturbed people, according to the writers or editors whose work I've read. Roz Avrett's protagonist, in "See No Evil," a *Redbook* story, spends one page telling us how tough it is to turn thirty-four and need bifocals. She gets them, though, and suddenly *sees* in new ways: her furniture is shabby, her walls the wrong color, her husband less attractive than she thought—"Maybe a hair transplant," she offers "brightly." But she does not shatter house or home. She permits her readers to suffer through her the shabbinesses of their own homes and then, like Dorothy returned from Oz, thinks (why she does we really aren't told) that "maybe the sight she needed was insight." So she gives up the bifocal contact lenses that made her see not wisely but too well, and she buys—truly—pink-tinted glasses. For the stale colors of her unsatisfying house, Acapulco Sunset and nubby Autumn Harvest plaid, "would be dynamite through rose-colored glasses." There's no place like home.

We are, if women, upset by the fact that our daughter is late coming home from school, according to "Running Past," by Jonellen Heckler, which appears in *Ladies' Home Journal*. It turns out that a girl-bully keeps standing before the little kid and not letting her cross the street. To discern this situation, we need a Momma. Pop is a well-meaning but imperceptive Dagwood, and when he comforts his daughter about the bully, she nods, but Mom knows "there is something else." There are two something elses: one is the child's, and the other is the cruel dilemma of the mother. We meet her as she is cooking. While she and her husband talk, she pours juice for him. She serves. But she wants "education," "delicious, tantalizing knowledge." She is going to sign up for a course, any course, at the local community college—not to get a job (she tells Jason, who could understand *that*), but for the joy of using her brain (he doesn't understand that). Suffice it to say that as the child learns to run past the bully, and learns that she really wanted to play *with* the bully as much as flee her, the mother learns, in spite of Dagwood, that she must both run-past and stay-with; going to school, she assures us, is not betrayal of your husband. *Is* it? Listen to the prose of the ending, and you might hear Norman Mailer breathing hard as he pushes us past psychic frontiers, or Nathaniel Hawthorne as he edges us into the dark forest of our national history and personal mystery: "At the mailbox in front of Hogan's Drugette I lift her up to flip the lid, and she drops the registration form into the mysterious darkness for me." She can be comforted perhaps by the worried declaration of these opening lines of "The Man Beside Me," a *Good Housekeeping* story: "Gran looked at me over her bifocals. 'There's nothing wrong with a woman having a career, just as long as it doesn't interfere with her having a husband and babies.'" Note those bifocals, for we're talking vision again.

We are not reading the exceptions here; we are reading the rule. That mysterious darkness, the palpitant hesitations, the trembling over Dagwood's obtuseness and the need to stay and pour him juice: this is the stuff that editors, who know about their readers, are choosing, and that writers, who know their editors (or whose agents know them), are sending in for selection. That is why it is so surprising to find in the same issue of the same magazine that printed "See No Evil," a *Redbook* story as accomplished as "Hollywood Starlet Tells All." It purports to be written by one L. Hluchan Sintetos. Who might be hiding behind the probable anagram, I am too unclever to know. But the writer shouldn't hide, for he or she has given us some good prose.

Why would the editors who picked all that stuff about Acapulco Sunset and balding hubbies pick this? It is a story of an actress who runs away from the press, from the director who dominates her, and from her own ambitions. She is, in other words, the stuff of national folklore, and her thighs are thinner than those of most of her readers, and she is supposed to have better sex than they, with more attractive men. But, so the national myth tells us, she is *really* unhappy. Just look at the screen magazines, or read the ostensible books by such alleged writers as Lauren Bacall: inside, you see, they are sensitive, these women; they are victimized by their success; and what they long to do is wear sneakers and sit on slipcovers made of nubby Autumn Harvest plaid. Your life ain't so bad, kiddo, the folktales tend to tell us; just look at mine. There's no place like home.

So, in spite of the vividness of Sintetos' prose, and the muscularity of the story, it is what Blondie needs to hear while Dagwood's away at the office. The director who finds our heroine hiding in Yuma is the kind of man who wears good clothes well, snaps his fingers for service, knows wines and wears an expensive watch. By their things, as I found out, you can know them. The director's portfolio is made of white ostrich skin and his initials on it are of gold. He is cold and cruel, is a second-rate filmmaker, and he victimizes the narrator: "'When you have filmed every inch of a woman, every expression of a woman,' he says, 'you know her like no other man has known her.'" She is Woman Not Her Own, as he is Svengali. In a publicity photo, she sees herself: "There it was: my image, larger than life and twice as plausible." She complains that it doesn't contain the real her: "my mother's death, the high school debating team, the St. Mary's Drama Club, the job at the center, my studio apartment fixed up with bed-sheet curtains." Like so many women on these pages and, presumably, like so many women reading these pages—according, I suggest, to their editors—she is only image, created by a man and manipulated by a man. Her recourse is to hide out and to starve. She is losing weight, she reflects, alone in the bathroom, "Ninety-three and still going down. Going down so fast that no one can catch me." Her only hope of escape is into herself.

There are, though, other escapes for troubled women in these pages of fiction. For some women here are troubled because they haven't yet become male-dominated images or mothers cooking for their kids while Dagwood is at the office. One can, according to "Tender Moments," Florence Jane Soman's *Good Housekeeping* story, get on board a trendy train and love her mother *to bits*. A nineteen-year-old woman falls in love one night. The big lug doesn't call her next morning. She confides in her reticent mother, and her mother confides back. They feel good: "My mother, Kay thought, my friend." Or the troubled woman can get pregnant, as in "Nine Long Months," a story in *McCall's* by Mary E. Ryan. A woman leaves her job at an art gallery, and her painting courses, because she is pregnant. Meanwhile, her Dagwood is made assistant manager of a computer-sales division in his company. They lose their sexual bonds: he is disgusted by her new physical condition and her eating habits—ice cream! she always wants ice cream! She mourns the death of their marriage and he stays away too late at a computer sales conference with a lovely companion. When they awaken, she finds, yes, *ice cream* in the freezer. He does love her! But there is actually no resolution, nothing happens that we didn't see happening, and the nothing that happens omits any sense of self-discovery on either partner's part, and surely it omits any sense of discovery of the partner.

So we are left with a story that seems to exist in order to state the problem. This is a story containing much reference to computers; the story itself seems to be another piece of technology, an instrument that exists to say the problem and do nothing more. Part of the process of taking back the happiness meant from birth to be yours might consist of sitting down and reading about other people who have the problems you do. I wonder if this is not part of the new anti-Freudian psychopiddle that began in the late sixties and flourished during the seventies, when it was stylish to be selfish, healthy, pretty and pretty much alone in your concerns. Part of the Me-First era is the birthright of enjoying oneself *now*, in selfish sex, selfish drugs, and selfish behavior. One lives in the present, alone, and the fiction of our time is often the fiction of the present tense in every sense. There is no narrative, in life or in art. Whereas Freud told us that the way to find health was to tell oneself and others the story of one's secret life, and to listen, the anti-Freudian narrative (of that time and this), as well as the behavior it studied or emulated, consisted only of *now; then*, along with explanations, causation, guilt or innocence, the murky channels of motive, all were dispensed with. Here, again, in "Nine Long Months," as in other cases nowadays, the story does not exist to tell us how or why: it is here to work like a tool, to say once more that there is a problem and that the problem hurts.

On the first page of Adele Glimm's "Something to Treasure," in *McCall's*, Clint the husband is the same basic, steady male figure as the husband in "Running Past" (the mailbox story). The wife is good at her public relations job, but endures, as she says, "the usual career-versus-child conflict." They are childless and she hungers for children. Clint is a *computer programmer*, and with their "borrowed" child, the daughter of Clint's sister, they all play at computer games. Their borrowed child will soon be taken from them to another part of the country. It seems that they will never have children. Nothing changes in the story, from beginning to end, except that the child will go, and they will go on. Again, the story is there to say their problem: it works like a small machine of limited function.

In bed, at the end, the couple don't make love; she is not ovulating, and it would not be useful to make love since she couldn't conceive— she calls it "impractical" love. The husband falls asleep and on his back she types, as on a computer keyboard, messages of love and cour- age. What dare we conclude? That the computer replaces intercourse of several sorts? (Ask the computer-kids who respond with vigor to machines but not to people.) That there is an American conflict be- tween the practical—love that does some *work*—and the purely plea- surable? Is this the other side of the anti-Freudian near-Onanism of which I spoke? We might well say *yes* to all these questions, and to this one too: Are stories in magazines like *McCall's* so scrupulously chosen and edited as to reflect the editors' sense of their readers? (Of course.) And, to continue: Does the recurrence of computers mean that editors know how much they can rely upon their readers' knowledge of them, for use in metaphors and as props and as, simply, the preferred new profession?

In the first serial publication of Ralph Lombreglia, "Goodyear," in *Atlantic*, there is much metaphoric use made of the Goodyear blimp, and of boozy, dope-y, antic pursuit and worship of the great, hanging ship. A scene from *Close Encounters of the Third Kind* is rehearsed at the end, and a kind of automatic despair from the first third of the story— " 'We're not fighting.' 'Whatever it is we're doing.'"—is matched by a mad mock-happiness at the story's close. Katy is invited to go to Flor- ence with a professor who is a satyr. She wants to go, because it "will mean a different caliber of dissertation—something that could end up as a book—and real chances for a job. She wonders why she wasn't this ambitious to begin with." Apparently her sudden ambition marks the death of love for our couple. Our hero has been invited to New York to work on making instructional video tapes. He's interested, and rhap- sodizes on his friends' studio: "It's full of astonishing technology— sublime, transcendental stuff. Everything in the place is on the com- puter. Everywhere you look, little red lights are flashing on and off as the machines remember things and make decisions." (But the prose makes clear, it's right to add, that, whether I happen to be moved by this story or not, Lombreglia can write.)

If stories can be machines for stating problems, they are also, as in

Vanity Fair, instruments by which the authors blow their own updated Aeolian harp. Ann Beattie's "Snow" tells us, "This is a story, told the way you say stories should be told"; it is an address by a woman to her former lover. At the story's sad end, the noncharacter narrator tells the noncharacter lover about how the snowplow clearing off their narrow road exposed "an artery," "though neither of us could have said where the heart was." It surely isn't in the story, which is about the author's pun, and not about the heart of either character, since neither lives on the page. The story is a tool of spooling words and meshing metaphors.

Computers are so very important to us. In "The Seduction of Peter S," an excerpt in *Penthouse* from the Lawrence Sanders novel, a man studying to be an actor starves. When he becomes a whore, "Business was brisk," we are told, and the protagonist considers computerizing his files. Watches make us tick, as we learned from Dick, the director and his Hollywood starlet; here, lighters fire up our sense of achievement: the actor's agent has a battered Zippo at the start, but as a pimp for actor-whores he later owns a gold Dunhill. Once art is left behind, there is *stuff* to celebrate: Burberry raincoats, fancy apartments, and the lie you can live with: "It *was* acting in a sense," the hero tells himself, as he names his bordello an "Academy of Dramatic Arts" so that the neighbors won't suspect. Academies, actors, drama, learning, and the notion that one might be more than either a raincoat-model or a penis, all are dealt with in this quite mechanical excerpt which, when it reaches for the language of high emotions, achieves this: "'My life hasn't exactly been a bed of roses,' she said casually. 'A lot of hard knocks. But I've gradually developed an instinct for the main chance.'" In a way, this fiction of sexual *realpolitik* is related intimately to the story of the housewife in her rose-colored bifocals: saying it makes it so, according to each; the story is the tool that services such needs. The people in such stories are little concepts summoned from cultural memory banks. They aren't people made dramatic or people portrayed metaphorically or people imitated in order that we be moved or entertained or, least of all, *changed.* Are we so cold, so used to the computer-selected situations and stick-figures of television, that these dead words about connect-the-dot situations are what we recognize? Or are we so horrified—by the world? ourselves?—that only numbing clichés are tolerable?

Dagwood's dream includes the black-dialect story, "No Trade," by James Howard Kunstler, in *Playboy*. It's about a team that's almost the

Yankees, run by an almost George Steinbrenner, and how an aging but accomplished black ballplayer becomes a metaphor for little people caught in big organizations. It's a revenge dream, the stuff that makes people read the *New York Post* for sports gossip. It is an American boy-man wish, wherein the Oscar Gamble figure can tell the Steinbrenner figure: "'If we wasn't who we was and where we is,' I tell him, 'I would unscrew your pointy little head like a forty-watt light bulb. . . . You are a liar through and through.'" Dagwood rises up in anger on the back of a black athlete: nothing more unusual happens, really, and little more is at stake; it's Sunday afternoon in the ballpark, and the boys are batting remarks instead of balls around.

The *Cosmopolitan*, where Hemingway almost fifty years ago de-scribed that boy-man? It features, among "Sexual Practices—A Siz-zling Update" and "I Married My Live-In Baby-Sitter," among the Hilma Wolitzer novel excerpt and the Laurie Colwin story, James Kunstler's "The Tie That Binds." This story begins with twenty-seven-year-old, single, Bethany finding a gray hair in her braid while living where "childless women dream of babies." Bethany, appearing in this magazine that purports to be about liberating the (female) self, declares that "men and women don't really *need* each other for any-thing but sex." But then she meets Tom, who is six-foot-four, thirty-two, and divorced. He's smart (he teaches geology at a university) and not a wimp (he "sells a little real estate on the side"). They move in together. They get married. They "begin to live as married people live in our part of the country." So all that's left out is the story, the people, and how and why they live as they do. It's a fairy tale for women tired of what *Cosmo* calls "Those Exhilarating Sexual Sprees"; it's a tool with which readers can fashion a prayer: "Oh, let me [her] stop mess-ing around and have kids in an Acapulco Sunset house."

Another magazine purportedly directed at women is *Playgirl*, in which that fine novelist, Herbert Gold, offers as a story "Seventeenth War or Revolution," about a nameless Veteran Journalist who suffers from Hemingway's ills—all of them: the *nada* problem, the woman problem, the battle-fatigue problem, the need-for-love problem, and of course the fear-of-love problem. He renounces the woman who loves him and whom he loves, and races through the airport carrying stuff, *tools*, "the lightest practical typewriter in the world banging at his flanks," instead of the woman who wants to do so. Like Huck, who flees civilization, the Veteran Journalist flees love because, like Huck, he has been there before and it was scary.

But note this: when he speaks of his emotional life, the Veteran Journalist calls upon word processors for his most useful analogue. The Journalist thinks, about his *soul*, "What they needed was something in the software to improve operations—replace whole paragraphs, correct spelling, regulate alignment." James Salter, in "Foreign Shores," published in *Esquire*, describes a man who has "something spoiled about him, like a student who has been expelled and is undisturbed by it." Not only are we dealing with wives who play their husbands' backs in bed like computer keyboards, and men who think of their lives as computers gone wrong, but we are dealing with the spoiled middle-class brat who practices expulsion like a faith. Salter knew that he could depend upon his audience to comprehend and respond to that analogue, as did Gold and Adele Glimm. Analogues exist to make clear, or amplify, aspects of a narrative that might, on their own, not flourish in the reader's mind. In order that an analogy work, the writer must, and the editor must trust that he succeeds at it, yoke the unfamiliar to the familiar. What is apparently unfamiliar, according to these writers, is a petulance unrelated to softness and wealth, or emotions untransmitted in "impractical love," as Ms. Glimm called it, or emotional turmoil in the middle years, as in Mr. Gold's story. We are those people, according to our authors, who respond to gold Dunhills, slim portable typewriters, computer keyboards, the software therefrom, and the edgy itching interior pucker of our something-like-souls that say we are incomplete unless we have a bundle in the bank, a baby in the womb, a husband on the run.

We must cherish a rerun, "Jailbird," by William Hazlett Upson in the revived *Saturday Evening Post*. It is one of the Botts/Earthworm Tractor Company epistolary stories that once, along with Tugboat Annie stories and Norman Rockwell covers, gave the *Post* its charm. Botts sells tractors, and he impressed a generation with the acumen he showed in being willing to do anything to move the merchandise: he was as much a representative of the American dream in 1961, when this story first appeared, as he is now. Here, he simply lies, bugs his competitors, breaks and enters, then steals, in order to get the order for his firm. "I was forced to fight fire with fire," he says, and the spirit of Richard Nixon rolls its shoulders with knotted glee.

Who stands against our darkness? It is, of course, William Saroyan, late and lamented and, in a *Post* story from his youth, quite typical in "The Miraculous Phonograph Record," as he shows how he and his mother refuted commerce and achieved a triumph on behalf of art. Is it significant that immigrants must record the victory? The recording is of a fox trot version of melodies from *Madame Butterfly*, played by Paul Whiteman, and it "had won over my mother to art, and for all I know marked the point at which she began to suspect that her son rightfully valued some things higher than he valued money, and possibly even higher than he valued food, drink, shelter and clothing." In the best sense of American art, and in contrast to the Sanders whorehouse tale or the Nixon tractor story, it is un-American.

Some of the fiction for September 1983 is literally not American. J. M. Coetzee's excerpts, in *Harper's*, from his January 1984 novel, *The War and Michael K,* is set in South Africa and is very much about that land. It is the powerful story of a brutally defeated man who is caught in a nightmare. Coetzee writes: "I am here, he thought, Or at least I am somewhere. He went to sleep." This marriage of Beckett and Kafka, like Coetzee's searing *Waiting for the Barbarians*, is very much in vogue now, not only because of its literary values, and perhaps least because of them. Stripped down and realistic, yet giving off allegorical resonance, this fiction is about the war between the human soul and the totalitarian state, the totalitarian impulse in the men who make the state. It is impossible for a right-thinking person to disapprove of such work. And because it portrays action in the larger, public sphere, which few short-story writers can or will do, the editors take excerpts from a novel and run them in the shape of a story; for their magazine is directed at people whose concerns are essentially sociological and political. This fiction, in other words, feels practical, and might appeal to readers who prefer nonfiction.

The *New Yorker* offers "The Jaguar Sun," by Italo Calvino, who has been ordained one of America's European Fictionists of the Moment. He was an interesting and innovative writer, and his early death is unfair. In this story, an intellectual travels and he makes notes. We're given lots of information about touring Mexico. An almost nonexistent woman, Olivia, whose passion for the narrator seems to be waning, discerns the importance of cannibalism in the primitive history that intrudes upon them. So the older man with the younger woman tries to create a possibility for passions of *mind,* for the functioning of sensualities not connected to sex. All this effort is based on the *aperçu* that the Aztecs were cannibals. He creates a metaphor for all life, and an excuse for living in the mind while pretending to live *la vie passionelle.* All is related to food, and at the end the dining lovers stare into each other's eyes "with the intensity of serpents," for they are aware "of being swallowed by the serpent that digests us all."

It's tough being a writer, out there on the circuit, middle-aged and waning, and young Olivia beside you cold as last year's reviews. In *Vanity Fair,* Philip Roth rehearses just how tough it is, and how the reviews of two decades past can still feel hot against a novelist's heart. "Just Point It and Fire It" is an excerpt from Roth's novel, *The Anatomy Lesson,* which concludes his Zuckerman trilogy.

Roth is one of America's consistently interesting writers, even when he fails sizably (*The Great American Novel*) or predictably (*The Breast*). For over twenty years he has talked essentially about himself and the experience of growing up Jewish, the belly laughs and sadness and anger of being Jewish and Philip Roth. His *Portnoy's Complaint,* part of which was first published in *New American Review* as "Civilization and Its Discontents," has become part of American mythology. So have the Jewish soldiers of "Defender of the Faith," the brilliant story in *Goodbye, Columbus;* so have Paul and Libby and Gabe and Martha of *Letting Go.* Roth's characters usually strike one as basically Roth or as derived from the landscape and fauna of his life. Thus, over the years, it is Roth's life, Philip Roth himself, that has, will he or nil he, become American literary folklore. And in his *Zuckerman Bound—The Ghost Writer, Zuckerman Unbound, The Anatomy Lesson* (and *The Prague Orgy*)—he meditates upon his middle years and revisits the grudges and delectations of earlier days.

In this *Vanity Fair* excerpt, Nathan Zuckerman is remembering his—and Philip Roth's—early literary career, and the critics who were cruel to him. It is Roth's life, and only the names have been changed to protect the author from the litigious. Thus, Portnoy is here called Carnovsky; *Goodbye, Columbus* is called *Higher Education;* the novelist Alan Lelchuk is Ivan Felt; and the critic Irving Howe is called Milton Appel, author of a critical attack "that doesn't sting just for the regulation seventy-two hours but rankles all his life." Zuckerman is not talking about a fictive review; Zuckerman is talking for Roth, and Roth is getting even, and the prose dies, after repeated poutings, a flabby death.

The language in this excerpt sounds less like the brazen jangle of Roth's galvanized, and galvanizing, music, and it seems more like the pedestrian and lip-bitten and temper-held workmanlike sentences of *Reading Myself and Others.* That collection of essays is essentially Roth's early defense of himself from those, usually Jewish, who attack him for writing fiction that Gentiles might use to further their anti-Semitic intentions. So the excerpt isn't in *Vanity Fair* for its beauty. Why then?

Why, because Philip Roth is rehearsing Philip Roth. Since his good work is literary folklore, and since Roth here points to the "real" people behind the attacks on Roth-Zuckerman, what we have here is *gossip.* This is the "12,000 Couples Share the Secrets of Intimacy," the "How Love Came Too Late for Jack and Jackie" of the *New York Review of Books* set. Much of this excerpt is like a savage cocktail party on West 86th Street in Manhattan at a quarter past six of an evening in fall. This is what *Vanity Fair's* editors think we want: gossip—which is really an extension of the data offered in *New Yorker* essays and *Redbook* advice, more technology, the material and tools one needs for improving oneself or for thinking that one is improved because the names and dates and dirty particulars are known, can be invoked, like shabby prayers, in order that the self feel somewhat less small.

There are other novels excerpted in September 1983 in our slicks— *Redbook's* Reeve Lindbergh Brown novel that ends with everyone attending the birth of a calf which seems to solve their problems, since the quarreling husband and wife "walked up the steps together and went back inside"; *Good Housekeeping's* "The Healing Touch," from the English Ann Knowles novel, wherein veterinarians, he and she, get together over animals and conclude their problems with the survival of a foal, while "somewhere in a far corner of the orchard, the first bird of the morning began to sing."

Whether or not we believe it really did sing, or whether we put our money on technology, and believe that the Goodyear blimp occasions possible love chosen over "a genteel, electronic life in media," we are dealing with a singular national literature thrown up on singular shores. Apparently, we want it. For we probably are, as the strange man wrote, "Damned strange people."

ᴥ THE FLOATING ᴥ
CHRISTMAS TREE

IT'S ALL TRUE: Greenwich Village, real poverty, heartbreak in the mails and famous writers in coffeehouses on Sheridan Square—"That's Thomas Pynchon!" "Who's he?"—and now that some years are between me and those days and I can look on them squarely, I am required to report that little has changed. I no longer live in Greenwich Village, it is true, but in upstate New York; my poverty is, like other truths nowadays, felt but relative; the mails still bring rejection, though less.

In 1963, Judy Burroughs and I were married, and we moved—she from a tiny town called Landisville, in Pennsylvania, where she taught, and I a few blocks from Charles Street in the Village—to 44A Morton Street. You walked through a wrought-iron gate between brownstones on one of the Village's serenest leafy streets, near the Hudson, and you passed a small garden and walked over flagstones to the first of two three-story wooden houses said to have been home to Aaron Burr's domestic staff.

We lived in the first house, on the ground floor. We could look through two windows onto the flagstone yard. Upstairs lived men who made a lot of noise and changed lovers with accompanying arguments and alarming information. One Sunday morning, sleeping in, the former Judy Burroughs of Pennsylvania and the former Freddy Busch of Brooklyn were wakened by a long, loud discussion in which the elements of lovemaking were minutely sketched by someone whose good friend was taxing his physiology. Grist for the mill, I thought. Judy, lighting a cigarette to simulate poise, set her hair on fire. Grist for the mill, I thought, after we beat the blue flames down.

Judy commuted to a Westchester school district from the Village, after some months, while I did very little besides look for work, find bad jobs and quit them. But from November through February, 1963 and 1964, we were office help in what was called market research. We, and a large number of out-of-work actors and writers, compiled data from forms filled out by users of experimental soapsuds. (People actually wrote that the product in question "made my wash come whiter, brighter," mimicking a TV ad of the day. Grist for the mill, I thought, as we labored long and singly. We had to pretend to be unmarried, since market-research firms thought couples an employment risk (fire one and the other would go sour on you). We cherished the fact of our marriage. It felt, on some winter nights, like a crucial secret we carried back into the darkness of Morton Street. We were ratified in marriage because we hid the name of marriage from the Philistines—who, not incidentally, did much to keep us fed.

We had seven dollars each week for food. Our rent was eighty-four dollars per month. Judy had four hundred dollars from her Pennsylvania retirement fund, and we brought in enough (thanks to the Philistines) to keep us going. For our first Christmas, we gave one another a single paperback copy of *The Family of Man.* I don't apologize for our sentimentality: we loved each other taxingly, hopefully, stupidly and dearly. We had no money for a Christmas tree because in the City anything that's vegetable and not dead costs more than a human life. I had stashed three dollars away, though, and at 11:45 on Christmas Eve, 1963, I stole out to Seventh Avenue where a man who sold trees for far too much sold me the runt of his litter (it came, at most, to my waist). Judy cut paper chains for it and I spent until 2 A.M. trying to fashion a stand from wood given, and tools lent, by Marie Alexander, who was janitor for our buildings and an accomplished painter with oil on canvas. I failed to build the stand, as I have failed to build nearly everything from 1963 to the present, so I strung wire and cord from each corner of the room, and I suspended the tree, using a bumbled bowline around its tip, in the center of my inept web. It was an artifice built of failure and affection, the best I could do. The tree floated and swayed, and the paper chains rustled, and Judy laughed, and it was a most excellent Christmas because we were what we had dreamed to be—in love, and undefeated in New York.

The room in which the tree swayed was the whole apartment. It was about 16′ by 16′. My boyhood bookshelves were our cupboards and counter. An industrial sink was nearby in the same corner of the room as our thigh-high refrigerator, attached to which was a waist-high stove with four gas burners, above which, attached, was our head-high oven. All were near the large stone fireplace, and to waken Judy for her long commute on winter mornings, since our small radiators rarely offered heat enough to stir the icy air, I had to turn the oven on and open its door after building a fire in the fireplace, with scrap wood found by Marie.

Crammed into our room was an armchair from Judy's apartment, and a table from her parents' dining room, and too many wooden chairs, and of course our double bed. I kept it covered with a red plaid blanket, for I was embarrassed lest strangers intuit its possible functions. Off our room was a bathroom, all ours, and very large. And there, at night, after our days of market research or job hunting, or rage—as on the day we quit a clerical job because the uptown vendor charged us ten cents for a candy bar instead of the universal nickel— there is where I wrote.

I had a portable typewriter, given me by my parents when I left for college. I sat on the edge of our enormous bathtub, rested the typewriter on top of the closed toilet, and, while Judy slept, I wrote. In those days I needed little sleep—I was twenty-two—and I was going to be a writer, I *was* a writer, I was going to get *them* to admit that I was a writer, and I sat in that awkward position and wrote my awkward prose. I was a failed poet. In graduate school, I'd admitted that I did not know where the poetic lines ought to end; I'd stopped ending them, had run them over from a justified margin, and had made prose narratives out of my terrible poems. But I still loved the music of poetry, and I tried still for poetry's concision, and its possibilities for a young man to sound like some Dylan Thomas of the short story. I larruped and looped, wove and wobbled, sank and rose and drifted on the languor of my lines. I was a very bad prose writer, and among the editors of magazines (and, later, books) in New York City, I was nicknamed Promising, and was rejected all the time.

I wrote more, because I knew that I was bright—my parents and my college professors had told me so—and because I knew that it was only a matter of time and mere fortune before I arrived. I wrote a story called "Myself, a Yielder," about a girl I had loved in Brooklyn in the late fifties. I couldn't know that I would not get it right until 1979, after it had grown from nine typed pages to forty, and had still been re-

jected by a dozen magazines. I wrote stories called "Alma Mater," subtitled "The Story of a Grocer." Always out of work, I wrote a story
called "A Job of Work." I wrote a story called "Going to Christmas." It
was about my mother, and it contained all the love and heartbreak
you'd expect of my mother's brilliant baby boy traveling with trepida-
tion into adulthood. Judy, wonderful friend, permitted me to send
twenty-five dollars—how had she helped us to scrape it up? where, in
those days, did such sums come from?—to the Scott Meredith agency.
Nobody, then, knew to advise me not to pay for a reading, so I sent my
twenty-page story off, and signed by Mr. Meredith himself, it said, a
two-page letter came back.

It said that only if his agency helped and encouraged new writers
could it "retain its place as a vital and thriving force in the community
of letters." I was nearly in the community of letters! "You qualify," the
letter told me, as a talented writer! "Your characterizations are excellent; your descriptive passages are evocative; your dialogue moves
smoothly along. . . . These virtues are commendable, and I think
you've got a lot of potential." And then the shoe, for which I'd been
waiting, fell: plotting, it seemed, was "your *bête noire.*" Mr. Meredith
addressed himself to plotting in general for some paragraphs before
going on to tell me that my story, in particular, was awful, so bad that
"I can't suggest a rewrite." So there I was. Call me Promising.

Judy told me to chuck the letter, suggesting that the letter was a
formula meant to entice me to send another story and another twenty-
five dollars. But what writer chucks *any* letter in which his name is
spelled correctly, in which he is recognized as having a lot of potential,
and in which it says that all he has to do is conquer the black beast of
awful and unrevisably inferior plotting? I put the letter in my Market
Information folder and Judy hugged me hard, as if to make up for what
I now think must have been resonances of doubt she felt in response to
Mr. Meredith's letter. But she didn't let on. She was, after all, the same
dear person who had sat in my apartment for hours as I wooed her by
reading her every story I had written. So I didn't surrender. I wrote
more stories—"Doris Day Loves Darwin," one was called, in which I
mastered the art of imitating the prose rhythms of Bernard Malamud
while showing none of his talent. I used an Irish name so that no one
would suspect I was copying him.

Shortly thereafter, I rediscovered Faulkner and went on to imitate
him. My first long work was a novella (really a novel gone dead) called

"There Is No Phenix." It might have been subtitled "A Kid from Brooklyn Rewrites *As I Lay Dying.*" But I wrote. Nearly every night, and often on Sunday afternoons—Saturdays were for Judy and me to sleep and to walk in the city—I did write. And a friend *did* point to a man, sitting with his back to us, reading a newspaper, in a coffee house called The Limelight—this was before it served liquor, when you could make a twenty-cent coffee last for all of that week's *Village Voice*—and say, "That's Thomas Pynchon." And I did not know who he was, nor did I care. I wanted people to be pointing to *my* back, saying *my* name. When asked, of course, I made it clear that my only interest in writing was the Service of Art.

We moved to Bedford Street in the Village—three rooms! a shower! a kitchenette!—and Judy started teaching in Westchester, while I began the first of several nasty writing jobs. For a while, I helped my first "publishing" employer—he and I were the firm—to plagiarize government documents, available free, into simpler English that might be useful to the Hispanic-American constituency my boss hoped to serve. I quit after two weeks. There were other jobs, and we had a more lavish Christmas in 1964, and then we moved out to Harrison, New York, where we lived without a car and, literally, on the wrong side of the New York Central tracks. Judy was closer to her work, and I to mine (by then I worked for a magazine in nearby Greenwich, Connecticut), and I wrote my first novel.

It was called *Coldly by the Hand.* I wrote it at night, after writing magazine-talk all day, and my brain was always mushy and words no longer sounded true—they were notes heard from too great a distance. But I wrote it every night, and I finished it, and I typed it all over, and I sent it off. And when Judy had helped me to discover that I despised the work I did, and that I wanted to return to someplace I thought safer for one's sense of language and for work that didn't make me feel ashamed, we moved from Harrison to Hamilton, New York, a couple of hundred miles up and toward the center of the state. And in my first week as teacher of freshman composition at Colgate—$6000 per year, and all the weekly themes I could eat—I had a letter from the Atlantic Monthly Press.

The immensely kind, decent, encouraging and gentle Esther Yntema of that house broke the news to me that my novel was rejected. She had encouraged me for nearly six months, and that sort of encouragement is underrated, usually by the writers who have received it, but it is stupendously important, and it still is given freely, and it goes far. You lie in bed at night, or walk across a windy campus, or lick at glue in an office with brown air, and you hear the phrase *enormous talent,* written by one who ought to know, and you are like a patient receiving plasma who feels the needle slide in: you know it's not all over, you know it is one day going to be wonderful, and you know that someone's caring for you—you are *not,* in a cruel profession, alone. I sent the rejected novel to other publishers and wrote two more books.

I would like to report this, now, because every writer dreams of it, and perhaps a new writer will see this story and know that it actually can happen. I had sent my third novel (the other two never have been, never will be, published) to a friend then living in Scotland. He is Robert Nye, a fine poet, novelist and critic now living in Ireland. His letters nourished me in 1965, when I started *Coldly* (the title is from a poem he wrote), and on through 1970, when I sent him my third novel, called *I Wanted a Year Without Fall.* Judy and I had returned from a trip to New York in February 1970. A friend had been at our house to care for our dog. She left us a note: one of us was to call Western Union. We did, and here's the message Western Union passed along: CALDER ACCEPTS YOUR NOVEL. CONGRATULATIONS. It was from Robert. It seems that he liked the novel and showed it to his publishers, Calder and Boyars, in London. Marion Boyars liked the novel enough to offer two hundred pounds. In those days, that amounted to $478. It took Mrs. Boyars from February until June to pay me for world rights to my book. I knew at the time that I was giving too much and getting too little, but I had no agent to lean on, and I had no strength for much resistance or negotiation—*it* was beginning, and I didn't want to do anything to jeopardize *it.* And though I was not to be published in America, by blessed New Directions and more blessed James Laughlin, until 1974, *it* had indeed begun. *It* didn't feel like an orchestra-backed moment in the movies, and there was surely no instant wealth, and, surely, there was less fame. But I was being published, after seven years of sending manuscripts out I was going to see a book of mine published, and Judy and I sat down in our shabby living room in our rented house and we got drunk, and more on the intoxicating release of pressure from those years' waiting than on the bite and burn of the cheap whisky we barely were able to afford and which we hardly remembered to swallow.

Two documents signify my young writer's life. The worst comes first. I read and reread it, in the early sixties and the late sixties and the early seventies, because it told me there was possibility even in what felt like whole failure. Harold Matson, who was Malcolm Lowry's agent—a generous one—sent it to him in 1941, saying, "I have regretfully come to the conclusion that I am not going to find a publisher for *Under the Volcano.*" The text of which I speak is the list that accompanied that note:

Farrar & Rinehart
Harcourt, Brace
Houghton Mifflin
Alfred Knopf
J. B. Lippincott
Little, Brown
Random House
Scribner's
Simon & Schuster
Duell, Sloan & Pearce
Dial Press
Story Press

These publishers declined an early version of that great novel. This list of them is owned by every writer I know, in his or her own analogous edition. For *Coldly by the Hand,* in a penmanship that looks familiar yet strangely young to me, inscribed in 1966 and 1967, I find this list:

Atlantic–Little, Brown	NO
Seymour Lawrence	
Assoc.	NO
David McKay Co.	NO
Atheneum	NO
Viking	NO
Putnam's	NO
Houghton Mifflin	NO
Scribner's	NO
Farrar, Straus & Giroux	NO

I acknowledged that my novel about two college professors I adored, and two young women I lusted after, was not quite *Under the Volcano.* But those parallel lists meant that we, Lowry and I, were brother sufferers and therefore brother writers. For we both, then, knew or had known the long pause, like the breath you take before ducking your head under water, and then its terrible extension, like keeping your head under water, and then its nasty conclusion, like being forced as you gasp for breath to go back under the water before you're ready. That was how it felt, sending the manuscript off, with its awful letter of clever chat. And then there was the waiting and speculating and fantasizing the book's acceptance, the book's *adoration*, and then getting back the usually polite and often graceful but always unambiguous *No*. Lowry's pain was curiously sustaining, then, and I returned to it for company. And perhaps it is worth adding, for those who do not believe in hope and perseverance and the need to *erode* resistance by raining one's work steadily upon the editorial soil, that the first firm on Lowry's list and the last firm on mine finally did publish novels by me in 1980 and in 1981: dreams can (almost) come true.

The other text is dated three years earlier—*Esquire* for July 1963. It was their writers-and-writing issue, and the best I've seen since I started to read the magazine. That was the issue which helped me to define the context of what I was beginning to see as a career. Gay Talese wrote of the expatriates of the fifties who fled to Paris "In Search of Hemingway." In those days, most young writers still were in search of Hemingway's genius, and some—I am among them—consider at least one of his novels and many of his stories to be as good as anything American fiction offers. So not only was I sniffing at the stoop of *Paris Review* and the *Deux Magots*, I was inhaling some second- or third-hand Hemingway; he taught us that the artist was a soldier on the page, a priest who had sex: we might dismiss the heady mix as youth, but we could not dismiss its seductiveness. Norman Mailer, Hemingway's Oedipal son in those days—art was the mother and wife—reviewed recent work by his colleagues, saying honestly how he saw them as adversaries in his Sweepstakes, and telling some fascinating truth about some misunderstood writers; his comments on James Jones's *The Thin Red Line*, and on postwar writing in general, still hold up. There were excerpts of works in progress (some of which still haven't seen light), and I felt, as I looked through the issue again and again, that I lived near the house of fiction, that I soon must find a way in.

Theodore and Renee Weiss gave me my first American publication in their *Quarterly Review of Literature* (in 1966); Wayne Carver was hospitable at *Carleton Miscellany;* and Ted Solotaroff, launching *New*

American Review, was warm and encouraging—he was the first editor to solicit my work and then to take some and then to pay a decent wage. And while there continued to be cruelty afoot, and stupidity, and editorial laziness; while editors couldn't read and wouldn't read—unless it was by Richard Brautigan or the author of *Love's Flaring Nostrils:* those were the literary poles; while an agent, Robert Lescher, did write to say that he liked my letter of inquiry more than the prose of my fiction—there nevertheless *was* scrupulous reading being given to serious writing, mine generously included. And editorial taste, for which there is precious little accounting, was in fact exercised with some conscience.

During the early days of *New American Review*, for example, Ted Solotaroff, now a senior editor at Harper and Row, received a story by Robert Stone. The story sent to Solotaroff is brilliant, it sums up a good deal of the sixties and of American romanticism, and it is a marvelous transmogrification: read an account of the actual incident in Tom Wolfe's *Electric Kool-Aid Acid Test*, and then see how Stone makes art out of madness in his "Porque No Tiene, Porque Le Falta."

Despite its quality, *NAR* was not always the first choice of many agents and authors. For during those days of the late sixties and early seventies, *Harper's* was publishing risky fiction and was paying well for it; *Esquire* was becoming a showcase for new writing; the *New Yorker* was stirred by some life. These were the places fiction went first, and then to *NAR*, and then to the smaller literary quarterlies (they could offer at most a readership of a few thousand, and not much payment).

So Stone's long story might well have had its last chance for reasonably wide readership and decent pay for its author when it was returned from *NAR*. Solotaroff rejected it. As he told me, he declined the story because it seemed excessively romantic. On the other hand, he said, he could not forget parts of it. An experienced editor, he listened to his inner voice and he sent for the story, then published it. This example of taste accounting for itself, and of grace notes sung louder than the music of woe, was sustaining at the time and remains so today.

Aspects of the taste for which there's—usually—no accounting became known to me in forceful personal terms when, in 1972, I wrote a short story called "Widow Water." I sent it to *NAR* and Ted Solotaroff sent it back. *Harper's* declined it next. Then Gordon Lish, the fiction editor at *Esquire*, rejected it. At this point, an agent took charge of my professional life and the story was sent to, and was sent back by, fiction editors at six other magazines.

In 1973, it went to *Paris Review* and George Plimpton accepted "Widow Water" and published it in 1974. In December of 1974, my agent received a letter from Gordon Lish, asking why he hadn't ever seen the story and wishing that he'd been given a chance to publish it. When told that he'd declined it two years before, he was amazed.

The story was reprinted in an anthology published in 1977, a time when I was finishing a novel and starting to assemble a volume of short stories. Like many writers who went from poems to stories to novels, I believe in economy—cut lines and paragraphs in fiction, even cut stories from collections. So I didn't include "Widow Water" in the original short-story manuscript I put together for my editor at Harper and Row. The collection was declined—"A collection of short fiction is not advisable for you at this stage of your career," I was told—and I went back to my Lowry list, not touched by such solicitude, and aware that story collections were actually, at times, scary to book editors. But I was luckier than many. My book of stories, *Hardwater Country*, was accepted by another house within two weeks. My new editor? The former fiction editor at *Esquire*, who had already published two stories of mine.

Lish and I prepared *Hardwater Country* for publication, and we decided that I'd cut too many stories. I brought six or seven with me to New York and Lish, after some hard reading, concluded that a story new to him, "Widow Water," should be added to the book. Lish read that story superbly, he edited it brilliantly, I honestly believe that he understood it better than I did. But it was brand new to him. And when I told him he'd seen it, he insisted that I was wrong. I didn't argue. It's nearly impossible to persuade an editor to convince his or her seniors to bring a book of stories out. This bright man was *volunteering*. I was grateful, despite the low advance and lack of any advertising, and I still am.

Hardwater Country was published. A reviewer for the daily *Times* savaged it, complaining of "modern fiction" in general and my brand of it in particular. He made it clear that the talkative and emotional plumber who narrates "Widow Water" was for him an example of "modern fiction" at its worst. Months later, when the book had already been returned to the warehouse, a reviewer in the *New York Times Book Review* wrote that "the best piece in this admirable collection is . . . a monologue by a plumber who performs his trade with the skill and sensitivity of an old-fashioned country doctor." Again: I was grateful, confused, and of course disappointed; my "doctor" apparently would live, but my book had died. And then there is this: in the *Times* the same daily reviewer, writing on his life in Connecticut some time after the publication of my book, wrote at length about his talkative plumber. A friend sent me the column, attached to a note which said, "Aren't you glad his pump got primed?" No, I wasn't, I have to confess. I still hated the feeling generated by serving as the source of a quotidian reviewer's comment on my own book (in small part) and a fuller exposition on the subject—usually him- or herself—that was of more interest to the writer holding forth in that day's paper. As my plumber might have said: the water that primes a pump is swallowed down, then swilled around in the pump's mechanical innards. As the pump begins to draw, the priming water is spewed up and out. A book that took years to make—never mind with what difficulties—becomes a mouthful of metal-colored spit.

One reason for telling this story is that in this profession there is little logic. Editors, dealing with art so very personally made, make personal decisions. There so rarely is or can be any accounting for their taste. To be sure, editors are fired, and for a variety of reasons. They are usually not fired, though, for letting interesting works of fiction that won't sell tens of thousands of copies slide from the slippery desk and back to their authors. Their life isn't easy, and despite jokes about editorial lunches, and despite one's disagreements with many editors' taste, there is good reason to fondly remember, say, Ted Solotaroff and Esther Yntema.

It came pretty true. We live in a farmhouse on a wild ridge above Sherburne, New York. Some of my neighbors know that I write things, and they don't hold it against me. Most of them don't know. From the back of our house, you can look over long fields to the town of Edmeston, and even toward Cooperstown. It is some of the handsomest rough country I know. On wonderful days I think more about the land, about our two sons, even about our awful cat and fine dumb dog, and of course about Judy, than I do about matters I call professional—the placing of my work in magazines and between hard covers and soft, and the terrible task of trying to manage whatever talent I was born with and energy I haven't squandered.

When I'm writing a book or story, I think about that work in progress all the time. And then I rarely, except when not sitting at the typewriter, think about the "professional" part. I call it that because what I do when I write is amateur—I do it for love, because of compulsive need, out of a requirement that I cannot shake: that I justify my time on the earth by telling stories. That's what I do. I have to do it.

But the "professional" part—the stuff people ask about after readings, the ugly information writers trade at awkward parties—I do because I love my amateur work and love some of what I've written and like a lot of it and even respect a quantity of it; it would be dishonorable to try less than my best on its behalf. (Before you snort with derision: of *course* I would like to be rich; of *course* I would like to be the Gary Cooper of American letters.) But when I write a story, I don't think, "Heh-heh! *This'll* grab 'em at *Playboy!* Have a little touch of Harold Robbins, guys!"

Indeed, I think that I do not think at all when I write. I sit at this battered, topless, sticky and chipped Royal 440 manual, and I type. He says, and then she says, and then they see something or hear it or learn it somehow, and then someone else makes her say to him what, it occurs to me as the story begins to close its arc and end, the story seems to have been wanting to be about. I think of myself as a jock, a verbal athlete. I move on the page in certain ways because long practice has taught me how to move best, and long needing has made me try to do it better, in new ways pleasing to my secret longings and the readers I do so very much want to reach and please.

I've written about children modeled after my children and about parents modeled after my parents. I have written about women I loved when young and—best: when I was really cooking at the Royal—about women I would love to love whether old, young or, as I now am, rather squarely in the middle. Readers who know me well have said that all my fictive women, no matter how imagined I insist they are, strike them as modeled, one way or another, near or far, after the former Judy Burroughs.

In *Rounds*, published in 1980, there's a woman named Lizzie Bean who is, I feel, cast away by my male protagonist, a doctor named Eli Silver. When I regretted recently to a friend that I had let Lizzie Bean be so poorly served, my friend said, "All women get cast away, Fred. That's why they keep ending up in novels." But I wasn't reassured. Because I modeled her physically and probably psychically after Judy my wife, I wanted to do better by Ms. Bean. I had to rescue her.

In the novel I've recently completed, *Sometimes I Live in the Country*, I pluck Lizzie Bean from the frozen fowl section of the Price Chopper supermarket in Bennington, Vermont, and I try to transport her to the sort of life she deserves. And of course it has to do, that life, with being at a farmhouse on a wild ridge above a place like Sherburne, New York. And Lizzie deserves a decent man with whom she can share what time she wishes to share. I haven't, therefore, given her a writer to love.

There's the economic reason, though I believe that Lizzie Bean, a working psychologist and independent woman, would not care about how little her fictive male friend might earn. But she would, surely, be displeased to live with a man who so wants attention, approval, a readership that, to him, is tantamount to *love*. For many writers, after a while, the only way the world, using its hard language, can assure them of its love, is by giving the writers money. It is what the world most begrudges the writer. When he receives currency, he knows that he is the possessor of the cruel world's heart.

Charles Dickens, one of the most energetic world-wooers, wrote about *Nicholas Nickleby*, first published in monthly installments: "the Author of these pages, now lays them before his readers in a completed form, flattering himself . . . that on the first of next month they may miss his company at the accustomed time as something which used to be expected with pleasure. . . ." In his preface to *David Copperfield*, he addresses "the reader whom I love." Dickens could never let his readers go; he always spoke to them, in his prefaces, because he left their company with such reluctance. He so wanted to be loved by his readers that he went out to meet them, giving dozens upon dozens of readings, in England and America, until he died as the result of an overexertion which was, I think, worthwhile to him. For he could stand before his readers and know, from their applause and their tears and their fainting into the aisles, that they loved him. Would Lizzie Bean's man-friend be different, except in degree, if he were a writer? I doubt it. How difficult it might be for Lizzie, then, to live with a man who, no matter how well he tried to love her, might be trying at least equally hard to woo a world of strangers.

And there is this reason, again exemplified by Dickens, this time on

his completion of *The Old Curiosity Shop:* ". . . writing until four
o'Clock this morning, finished the old story [in which Little Nell dies].
It makes me very melancholy to think that all these people are lost to
me for ever, and I feel as if I never could become attached to any new
set of characters." It couldn't lessen difficulties for Lizzie if she knew
that Dickens deeply mourned the passing of each set of characters:
he expresses the "reluctance and regret" he feels in leaving "my vi-
sionary friends" from *Martin Chuzzlewit;* he sorrows painfully over
Paul Dombey's death in *Dombey and Son;* the man whose wife—he
threw her out, Lizzie, for a younger woman, an actress!—bore them
ten children refers to *David Copperfield* as his "favourite child." Lizzie
would be living with a man who passionately loved his characters and
those strangers he required for audience. That is a good deal of competition, even for a woman as strong and attractive as Lizzie. (She is *so*
strong, you may have noted, that I am writing about her as if she is
true. If circumstances may be tough for Lizzie Bean, how easy can
they be for Judy Busch?)

And then there is this for Lizzie to consider: so many writers are
self-lovers even more than they are lovers of their characters or readers. In the making of art, after all, lie so many possibilities for the
making of love to oneself; writing can be a frictive as well as fictive
experience. One is listening to oneself because one is doomed to, from
birth, if a writer; the process of surviving in that profession, with such
a curse of inwardness *and* outwardness, is one of learning that a seam-
less fusion of inner and outer worlds produces art; the rest is either
masturbation, if too much inner world dominates, or good journalism,
if the outer world holds sway. The danger is that one must invite as
much as possible of each world into the mind and onto the page (at
least in early drafts). But all too frequently, the writer can forget to
listen to everything except the self—it speaks so sexily. Writing, then,
is a test of character; the ones who pass are merely doing what their
trade requires, while the ones who fail are doing what comes, alas, quite
naturally. An acquaintance of mine, a writer whose work is published
often enough, assures us, in a published interview, of "the world of
emotional extremity" in which he lives, adding rather exquisitely that,
while "all people walk over it," only he and his fellows-of-sensibility
"are doomed to live there." He says that "the pain, frustration and
torment of this calling takes its toll." Imagine, then, that Lizzie Bean
comes home from a tough two hours with a depressive. She and her

male friend pour out drinks, sit in the living room, and begin to trade stories in the ordinary domestic debriefing that goes on between mates. Lover-boy suddenly wags his pipe at her and impatiently shakes his head, requesting silence: she may have "walked over" the terrain of emotional extremity, he tells his beloved, but *he has been living there*, don't forget, just on the other side of the psychic toll booth.

No. I'm too much of a realist to want to write a potential self-lover into the life of a woman who needs some company. I'm too much of a lover of my own characters to want Lizzie Bean living with a man who might love his characters or his public or the nauseous sentimental self more than he loves her. I'll not let her love a writer.

And, while I've dared to imitate aspects of my wife in order to make a Lizzie Bean whom I can love, though she mustn't love the likes of me, I have worked at *not* writing fiction about the first Christmas together of me and the former Judy Burroughs. I think that I am waiting for the right—the perfect—fiction for that image, a context in which that wonderful ugly tree, tied, in the air, to the corners of our first apartment, can be useful in a grand story while it remains completely the runt Christmas tree of 1963. Fiction writers are sworn by the nature of their work to such fealties. They deal with matters of the earth, with objects of specific gravity. I believe that I and my brothers and sisters in writing strive to keep our feet as firmly on the ground as Judy's Christmas tree and mine was off it. I believe that we remain writers because we return to that striving each time—as here, now—we fail.

✦ INDEX ✦

84, 85, 90, 92, 93, 95, 104, 133
"Hawthorne and His Mosses," 84
Hayford, Harrison, 93
"The Healing Touch," 142
Heart of Darkness, 21
The Heart of the Matter, 27
Heckler, Jonellen, 132
Hemingway, Ernest, xiii, xiv,
 xviii–xix, 5–6, 10, 12–13, 16, 24,
 27, 29, 82, 97–101, 102, 104, 107,
 110, 130, 138, 150
"His Last Bow," 63
Holt, Victoria, 24
Household Words, 45, 47, 52
Housman, Laurence, 29
Humors of Blood & Skin, 108, 109
Hunger, 35–36

"I and My Chimney," 87
The Innocent Party, 102
In Our Time, 12, 27
Invisible Mending, 29
Israel Potter, 93

"The Jaguar Sun," 140
"Jailbird," 139
James, Henry, 104
Jones, James, 150
Joyce, James, xv–xix, 7–8, 15, 22, 98

Kafka, Franz, 31, 33–36, 38–42, 89,
 140
Karl, Frederick R., 16–17
Kennedy, William, 17
King of the Jews, 26, 112
Kinnell, Galway, 9
Knowles, Ann, 142
Kunstler, James Howard, 137–138

L'Amour, Louis, 131
Last of the Just, 26
Lawrence, D. H., 1
Letting Go, 141
Levine, Philip, 9
*The Life and Adventures of Martin
 Chuzzlewit*, 46, 156

*The Life and Adventures of Nicholas
 Nickleby*, 46, 155
The Lime Twig, 102
Little Dorrit, 37
Locke, John, 90
Lolita, 15
Lombreglia, Ralph, 136
The Longest Journey, 37
Losing Battles, 10
Lowry, Malcolm, 15, 23, 41, 149, 150

Macbeth, 51
McCarthy, Cormac, 18
McElroy, Joseph, 16
Mailer, Norman, xiv, 65–68, 69–70,
 71–82, 133, 150
"The Man Beside Me," 133
"The Man Who Studied Yoga," 65,
 66, 68, 72, 74–75, 76, 77
Mardi, 83
The Mayor of Casterbridge, 21
Melville, Herman, xiii, 15, 16, 17, 23,
 31, 32, 38, 66, 68–69, 70–75, 79,
 81, 82, 83–96, 116
Memories and Adventures, 56
Memories of My Father, 54
The Metamorphosis, 31, 34
Milton, John, 16
"The Miraculous Phonograph Rec-
 ord," 140
Moby-Dick, 15, 23, 66, 68–69, 72–
 73, 75, 79, 83, 84, 88, 116
A Moveable Feast, 13
"MS. Found in a Bottle," 92
Murray, Albert, 10

Nabokov, Vladimir, 15
"The Nearest Cemetery," 101
Nickel Miseries, 27
"Nine Months Long," 134, 135
"Notes on Writing a Novel," 104–105
"No Trade," 137–138

"An Odor of Chrysanthemums," 10
Of a Fire on the Moon, 80
O'Hara, John, 14